"Sometimes books make you feel [...] better. This one does both. *Lovin[g...]* us to put down our phones, cross t[...] carpool line, and rediscover sponta[...] keen insights into our personal an[...] [...] make her the perfect person to speak into how we can shift our lives from disconnected to connected with the people right around us every day. If you want life to be less busy and more meaningful, this is your book."

Krista Gilbert, author of *Reclaiming Home* and cohost of *The Open Door Sisterhood* podcast

"In a culture saturated in all things 'social,' we've become isolated and too busy for each other in real life. We know more about strangers we've never met than the people we see every day, walking their dogs, playing with their kids, or waving hello as they drive by our house. In *Loving My Actual Neighbor*, Alex Kuykendall shares her own story of stepping out of her comfort zone and learning how to love those around her with more intention. With honesty, humility, creativity, and transparency, Alex gives us seven practical and biblical steps to lean into relationships right in front of us so that we can experience the beauty of authentic, grace-covered neighboring and community. I highly recommend this book!"

Renee Swope, bestselling author of *A Confident Heart* and former radio cohost, Proverbs 31 Ministries

"We have an opportunity to send the world a message of hope by caring for the people right around us. *Loving My Actual Neighbor* is a great resource for any Christian who is wanting to do better at building relationships with those not already in their immediate circles. It offers practical approaches to connecting with our neighbors, our officemates, and the person we find standing next to us on the soccer sidelines. Alex is the real deal, and she lives out the content of this book in her everyday life!"

Dave Runyon, coauthor of *The Art of Neighboring*

"Do you love your neighbor? Or do you not know her name yet? Many of us *theoretically* believe in loving our neighbor, but when life gets busy the reality is it's hard to remember her name. Learning to care about and love the person right next to you can be a life-changing journey. Alex Kuykendall's *Loving My Actual Neighbor* is an encouragement to reach across the fence, open up your heart, and build a connection in the relationships right in front of you."

Claire Díaz-Ortiz, author and speaker, ClaireDiazOrtiz.com

"*Loving My Actual Neighbor* inspired me, guided me with insightful ideas, and left me wanting to love Jesus more. A very practical and needed voice to help women do real ministry. I hope women will read this book, take it to heart, and, of course, share with their neighbors!"

Sally Clarkson, author of *The Lifegiving Home* and host of the *At Home with Sally* podcast, SallyClarkson.com

"In a time and space where it's easier for us to surround ourselves with those who look, think, and vote like us, we need tools to help us engage with and authentically love those who may not. Taking Jesus's command to love our neighbor seriously means doing the hard work, it means sacrifice, and it requires a retraining of our brains to enter into relationships of mutuality with one another, where we can genuinely say you need me and I also need you. With personal experience and practical insight, Alex Kuykendall guides us through this process."

Vickie Reddy, executive producer, The Justice Conference

"Let's be honest. L-O-V-E is a four-letter, power-packed word that can be so hard to show to people we live with, much less someone we barely know! Alexandra Kuykendall reminds us of the importance of drawing close to people instead of pulling away, to choose love especially when we don't feel like it. And most of all she reminds us that sometimes we need to simply see past our assumptions and fears, get up, knock on a neighbor's door, and just say hello!"

Maggie John, host and senior executive producer, *100 Huntley Street*

"In a world searching for connection, Alexandra Kuykendall takes us by the hand and walks with us through the uncertainties, anxieties, and inevitable neighbor fails of learning to belong to the people near us. This book is full of practical ideas for anyone longing for true community but too nervous to open the door. Where do we start? Right here."

Shannan Martin, author of *The Ministry of Ordinary Place*

"A book has never been more needed than this one! Refreshing and practical, it helps us approach loving our neighbors with humility and connection. It's actually how I think Jesus might love if he lived next door today. These pages are helping us take giant steps in all the little ways of practicing love right in our own communities. And that has potential to change the world!"

Sarah Harmeyer, founder and chief people gatherer, Neighbor's Table

Loving My Actual Neighbor

Other Books by Alexandra Kuykendall

The Artist's Daughter
Loving My Actual Life
Loving My Actual Christmas

Loving My Actual Neighbor

7 Practices to Treasure the People Right in Front of You

Alexandra Kuykendall

BakerBooks
a division of Baker Publishing Group
Grand Rapids, Michigan

Published by Baker Books
a division of Baker Publishing Group
PO Box 6287, Grand Rapids, MI 49516-6287
www.bakerbooks.com

Printed in the United States of America

Library of Congress Cataloging-in-Publication Data
Names: Kuykendall, Alexandra, author.
Title: Loving my actual neighbor : 7 practices to treasure the people right in
    front of you / Alexandra Kuykendall.
Description: Grand Rapids : Baker Publishing Group, 2019.
Identifiers: LCCN 2018043258 | ISBN 9780801075377 (pbk.)
Subjects: LCSH: Love—Religious aspects—Christianity. | Neighborliness—
    Religious aspects—Christianity.
Classification: LCC BV4639 .K88 2019 | DDC 241/.4—dc23
LC record available at https://lccn.loc.gov/2018043258

Unless otherwise indicated, Scripture quotations are from the Holy Bible, New International Version®. NIV®. Copyright © 1973, 1978, 1984, 2011 by Biblica, Inc.™ Used by permission of Zondervan. All rights reserved worldwide. www.zondervan .com. The "NIV" and "New International Version" are trademarks registered in the United States Patent and Trademark Office by Biblica, Inc.™

Scripture quotations labeled ESV are from The Holy Bible, English Standard Version® (ESV®), copyright © 2001 by Crossway, a publishing ministry of Good News Publishers. Used by permission. All rights reserved. ESV Text Edition: 2016

Scripture quotations labeled MSG are from THE MESSAGE, copyright © 1993, 1994, 1995, 1996, 2000, 2001, 2002 by Eugene H. Peterson. Used by permission of NavPress. All rights reserved. Represented by Tyndale House Publishers, Inc.

Scripture quotations labeled NASB are from the New American Standard Bible® (NASB), copyright © 1960, 1962, 1963, 1968, 1971, 1972, 1973, 1975, 1977, 1995 by The Lockman Foundation. Used by permission. www.Lockman.org

Scripture quotations labeled NLT are from the *Holy Bible*, New Living Translation, copyright © 1996, 2004, 2007, 2013, 2015 by Tyndale House Foundation. Used by permission of Tyndale House Publishers, Inc., Carol Stream, Illinois 60188. All rights reserved.

Some names and details have been changed to protect the privacy of the individuals involved.

19 20 21 22 23 24 25   7 6 5 4 3 2 1

In keeping with biblical principles of creation stewardship, Baker Publishing Group advocates the responsible use of our natural resources. As a member of the Green Press Initiative, our company uses recycled paper when possible. The text paper of this book is composed in part of post-consumer waste.

green press INITIATIVE

For Derek

You teach me to be a better neighbor.

I watch and learn.

Contents

Contents

More Ways to Connect with Your Neighbors

Acknowledgments   215

Notes   217

Introduction

A Framework for Loving Your Neighbor

Do not waste time bothering whether you "love" your neighbor; act as if you did.

As soon as we do this we find one of the great secrets. When you are behaving as if you loved someone, you will presently come to love them.

C. S. Lewis, *Mere Christianity*

"Teacher, which is the greatest commandment in the Law?"

Jesus replied: "'Love the Lord your God with all your heart and with all your soul and with all your mind.' This is the first and greatest commandment. And the second is like it: 'Love your neighbor as yourself.' All the Law and the Prophets hang on these two commandments."

Matthew 22:36–40

I didn't even know her name. Those words repeated in my head as I pictured the young woman who had lived across the street from us the last few years. Like me, she had young children: a preschooler and a baby. That detail alone offered all kinds of potential connection points. From sleepless nights to intense love, two women can bond over the roller coaster of parenting littles. However, our relationship never got past a quick smile and hello as I would walk by her house. Instead of stopping to chat, I would avert my eyes and keep walking.

What kept me from stopping all those times I walked by? Her kids in the plastic kiddie pool in their front yard offered the most natural conversation starters. Why hadn't either one of us pushed through a little bit of the awkward and introduced ourselves? Why didn't we ever move from two neighbors who didn't know each other to those who did?

Was it the nature of mothering young kids? We were both busy and exhausted and could only carry on conversations in ten-second spurts with the constant interruption of running after children in the street, so was it not worth the effort? Was it personality? No one has ever accused me of being an extrovert. Or did our differences consciously or unconsciously keep us from taking that initial step toward the other?

Though our kids were roughly the same ages, my neighbor appeared to be ten to fifteen years younger than I, perhaps entering motherhood as a teenager. She was a different race, wore different clothes, and, based on what was blasted into her front yard, listened to different music. In terms of proximity, she lived as close as anyone, but in some ways her life felt foreign to mine. She and her husband (or boyfriend?) hosted parties into the early hours of the morning, their equally young friends keeping us up with their yelling, laughing, and music. I wondered if most of their late-night guests still lived with their parents, making our neighbors' home the party house by default. On hot summer nights I would close our bedroom window to keep the noise out, which as a result kept the heavy air in. Turning from side to side on the sheets, I thought about how precious my sleep was. In the mornings it was easier to be angry, or at best indifferent, than friendly. That indifference should have been a clue that my attitude needed some adjusting.

The questions of why we didn't connect still linger. I'll never know the answers to them because one day she was gone. There was a flurry of police activity at their unit and a devastating family crisis, and I never saw her again. It bothered me that I couldn't even pray for her by name. I recognized an opportunity lost. Not that any increased friendliness on my part would have changed her situation, but everyone can use a little extra support right where they are. My guilt was more acute because of my day job. I was working at MOPS (Mothers of Preschoolers) International, one of the largest mothering ministries in the country, writing and speaking on the importance of reaching out to isolated moms of young kids. It did not escape me that the mother of a preschooler living closest to me, my *actual neighbor*, was in crisis and I did not know her. My pastor, Steve, says, "Jesus walked toward people." I'd failed at walking across the street toward my young neighbor.

It was a wake-up call of sorts. It took a crisis and regret for me to examine my resistance to loving my actual neighbor. I don't want to wait for another crisis before I show the people right in front of me that they matter.

Why a Book on Loving Your Neighbor?

I'm writing this book because I need it. I want to love my neighbors. After all, in many ways it is our main job description. But when it comes to the how of loving the people right next to me, especially those I may not find easy to even like, I often don't know where to begin.

I'll start right off by letting you know what I am not. I'm not a pastor or a theologian. I'm not a reporter or a social worker. Nor am I a counselor or a professor. I am, however, a kitchen anthropologist, stationed smack-dab in the middle of the United States. From my kitchen in Denver, I watch a world of disconnection around me. In families, churches, and communities, we are missing each other. Often our intentions are good, but we get stuck. At least I do.

The honest truth is I go about my days with my agenda, maintaining my priorities and my comfort. My default is to protect what feels good, safe. Unconsciously, I avoid discomfort. A mother of four, I live an overscheduled, distracted life. When I think about loving my neighbors, I wonder what it will cost me as far as time and energy, both of which feel maxed. Not to mention my worries about if we'll relate, what we'll talk about, what they'll think of me, if it will be awkward (even contentious), and whether it will feel more like work than friendship. Despite these self-focused hang-ups, I know *it's not all about me*. That's the idea behind loving our neighbors, right? That we move past our agenda, comfort, and convenience and toward love. So I'm willing to dive into this topic to learn.

Unlike my other books with similar titles (*Loving My Actual Life* and *Loving My Actual Christmas*), this is not a journaled account of an experiment. Rather, this book contains stories, ideas, and practical tips that can inspire and help us. I'm glad you're on this journey with me.

Why This Book Now?

We find ourselves in unique times characterized by words like *polarization*, *isolation*, and *conflict*. In some ways we are collectively hitting, or at least approaching, a crisis of inter-personal connection. Though we are more connected to the world through information than ever before, the need for increased face-to-face interaction is evident. Whether young or old, Americans are feeling more isolated. According to a recent study from the Pew Research Center, about half of Americans have weekly interactions with their neighbors, which means half of us don't.[1] A survey by AARP found about one-third of respondents over the age of forty-five are lonely.[2] And according to the American Psychological Association, loneliness and social isolation have similar effects on health as obesity and can lead to premature death.[3]

No surprise, social media doesn't help the feelings of isola-tion. We can have serious fear of missing out (FOMO) when it seems we aren't invited to the places everyone else is (or even have the same number of likes or comments as someone else). The opposite is also true. When we replace a virtual meet-up with a real one, we can decrease our actual isolation.

Not to mention the tension that exists in the political cli-mate of our nation and world. It seems gone are the days when families can sit down and have civil dinner discussions about different political views. The combination of real and per-ceived isolation, with an increased tendency toward extreme language and huddling in our like-minded, like-living tribes, is not moving us in the direction of unity. Rather, it's contributing to a "me vs. you" and "us vs. them" mind-set. Not exactly the atmosphere of welcoming and loving the stranger.

Jesus's commands don't change with the political tides, but they certainly sound more poignant under certain circumstances. We are being set up culturally to do what Jesus told us, in a way that will make his mercy and grace more evident to the world. At the Last Supper, as Jesus was preparing to leave his disciples to complete his assignment on the cross, he said,

> Let me give you a new command: Love one another. In the same way I loved you, you love one another. This is how everyone will recognize that you are my disciples—when they see the love you have for each other. (John 13:34–35 MSG)

These are essentially Jesus's instructions for his followers as he left this earth. It seems we should pay attention to them.

Who Is My Neighbor?

A neighbor can be the person with the address adjacent to mine—the next stop on the mail carrier's route, if you will—but it can also be the person on the other side of town or the other side of the world. In this global era our interconnected lives allow us contact with those who are not in our own communities. Our "neighbors" are indeed on every corner of the globe.

However, in this book I will be using the term *neighbor* to refer to those who are near enough to see, touch, smell, and hear in person, because these relationships offer some unique dynamics. There is something about being in someone's physical presence that is different from seeing them on a screen or reading about them. So though I have many "friends" on Facebook, who do I call when I'm locked out of my house or need to drop my kids off while I head to the emergency room? My neighbors—the people who are right in front of me.

I will also be using the term *neighbor* as separate from family or friends. I am narrowing in on those people who aren't automatically on our texting rotation. It could be a coworker who is difficult, a next-door neighbor we wave to but whose name we can't remember, the school secretary, the older guy at church who doubles up on the cookies. In other words, my neighbor is not my bestie.

Why These Seven Practices?

Jesus's words about loving my neighbor were rattling inside my head when my friend Karen Parks and I met for a quick lunch last summer. We never lack conversation topics, because we both have a tendency to make connection points between any two subjects. Truly, try us. So over noodle bowls we jumped from one topic to the next and the next, barely pausing to breathe because there's so much still to talk about. I brought up this topic of what it means to love our neighbor, and she suggested a spot in 2 Peter.

"There are some verses in the first chapter of 2 Peter that I don't think get enough attention," she said. She then laid out their premise—the verses are a framework for building relationships with our neighbors, much like when we're building a house. There are some foundational elements that help us move toward generous love that we shouldn't skip over. She emphasized that a strong foundation helps sustain us when things get hard and the initial enthusiasm about the idea wears off. In other words, we need this foundation if we are to be committed to loving our neighbors in terms of years rather than days or weeks.

I made a note on my phone, and the next day I looked the verses up again. Yes, Matthew 22:36–40 directs us to love God and love others. But these verses from the first chapter of 2 Peter give a fresh perspective on the how:

> For this very reason, make every effort to add to your faith goodness; and to goodness, knowledge; and to knowledge, self-control; and to self-control, perseverance; and to perseverance, godliness; and to godliness, mutual affection; and to mutual affection, love. For if you possess these qualities in increasing measure, they will keep you from being ineffective and unproductive in your knowledge of our Lord Jesus Christ. But whoever does not have them is nearsighted and blind, forgetting that they have been cleansed from their past sins. (vv. 5–9)

Eugene Peterson's paraphrase *The Message* says it this way:

> So don't lose a minute in building on what you've been given, complementing your basic faith with good character, spiritual understanding, alert discipline, passionate patience, reverent wonder, warm friendliness, and generous love, each dimension fitting into and developing the others. With these qualities active and growing in your

lives, no grass will grow under your feet, no day will pass without its reward as you mature in your experience of our Master Jesus. Without these qualities you can't see what's right before you, oblivious that your old sinful life has been wiped off the books. (vv. 5–9)

Peter was writing to encourage growth in both Christian faith and consistent practice.[4] He starts with faith as the baseline. He does not, however, say how long someone must believe or how they came to faith, mention their lineage, or require other qualifications. So we are to assume that this directive is indeed for anyone who follows Jesus. That's us!

When I considered the instructions in these verses, I couldn't help but think of the reflections I'd heard from people I interviewed while researching this book, people I know who step over potential barriers to love their neighbors well. I'd noted some common themes in their observations of the church and how we interact inside and outside our proverbial walls. And now I could see how these verses provide a framework for living out the Christian life in a way that cares for our neighbors. Seven practices emerged from both the verses and my research:

1. Holding a posture of humility
2. Asking questions to learn
3. Being quiet to listen
4. Standing in the awkward
5. Accepting what is
6. Lightening up
7. Giving freely

Though Peter didn't necessarily intend for these elements to build on one another, they do. They have a natural crescendo, and so we will look at them in the order Peter presents. Taken together, they give us a full picture of *how* our faith can be practiced in a way that will impact those right in front of us with respect and genuine care.

A practice is something someone tries that they can and should repeat in order to get better. Like so many things, muscle memory is involved. For example, when one of my daughters works at mastering a new passing skill in soccer, it is awkward at first. She requires some instruction and guidance on how to try it out, and she works at it over and over until she doesn't have to think quite so hard on it. The skill comes a little more easily and a little more instinctively with the work. Though she improves, she always has potential for further improvement. In other words, she never completely masters it, so she continues to practice.

As you consider these practices, know I am right there considering them with you and thinking through how we as Jesus followers can implement them. I call this "Saturday living"—connecting our neighbors' (and our own) difficult realities with the truth that Christ has come to set us free.

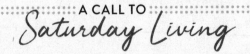

A CALL TO
Saturday Living

A neighborly life marinates in the Saturday life. Saturdays are for mowing the lawn, hanging out on the sports sidelines, and heading to the grocery store. They are days of proximity, with natural interactions happening all around us. In the context of these interactions, relationships with our neighbors can develop . . . or not. It is up to us to decide if we will take these opportunities to put the seven practices into place or if we will allow them to slip away. Whether our Saturday life is spent in work or play, we've been placed in our unique communities at this time in history with our specific neighbors. From the office cubicle to the swing at the park playground, we find ourselves at points of time throughout our day that no one else can claim. Our neighbors—the people right in front of us—are not those we choose, but those we can choose to treasure.

There is another element to Saturday living, a tension we hold as Jesus followers that is found most profoundly on Saturday—Holy Saturday, that is. We are people defined by the resurrection. We know the hope of Jesus overcoming death, and yet our days are found in a fallen world in the shadows of Good Friday. Life on this earth is in the Holy Saturday space. The in-between. The grief on one side of us and the freedom yet to come on the other. As pastor and author Tony Campolo is famous for saying, "It's Friday . . . but Sunday's coming."[5] While we stand in the Friday pain of the world, we have the Sunday knowledge of the hope found in Christ. We are to operate out of both. This is Saturday living.

In a way, we are very much tethered to both sides. Our incarnational selves walk through our own aching and grief, and our souls sing the praises and promises of heaven. It is in this tension that Jesus calls us to truly love our neighbors—to not shy away from the difficulties, even grittiness, of life with them, all the while holding the good news on their behalf and for them to see. Our larger goal when loving our neighbors is to be hope bearers. Everything we do and say, every practice we practice, is with the end goal of portraying Christ's hope in a hurting world. It is here that Saturday living with our neighbors can happen all week long.

As we begin this journey together of exploring how to love our neighbors well, may we remember that God's grace is covering it all. We are imperfect people stumbling through life, trying to love other imperfect people. If we are getting more honest in relationships, there will be moments (or days or weeks or years) that will be difficult. Things won't go as we picture they will. The mess will seep out and we will miss opportunities that come up. We will likely say things we regret, and we will face feelings and ideas that make us uncomfortable. But we will also experience life as God intended with more depth as we interact with those right in front of us on a more intentional level.

Jesus was 100 percent clear: love God, love others. May we do so in a way that is honoring to both our Creator and those he created, with respect for all involved and dignity in every interaction. May our motives be genuinely connected to our belief that God loves people and wants us to flourish. May we lock arms as the church and determine to love our neighbors. Not because they've earned it, not because we owe them something, but because they are here and God calls us to it.

Questions for *Reflection*

1. When have you felt well loved by a neighbor? How common is it for you to experience neighborly love?

2. Do you feel the need to love your neighbor out of responsibility (you know it's what you must do) or out of desire (your heart is compelling you in this direction)? Or both?

3. Who do you see as your neighbor?

4. Looking ahead at the practices discussed in the book, which do you think will feel most natural for you? Which practices do you predict will offer the biggest challenges? Why?

5. How do you currently hold the hope of Sunday for your neighbor? Does the reminder of Holy Saturday offer a helpful picture for you? Why or why not?

Scripture to *Digest*

So this is my prayer: that your love will flourish and that you will not only love much but well. (Phil. 1:9 MSG)

1

Holding a Posture of Humility

Be humble. The world is bigger than your view of the world. And certainly, God is much bigger than your view of God.

Eugene Cho

When pride comes, then comes disgrace,
but with humility comes wisdom.

Proverbs 11:2

My husband, Derek, and I moved into our Denver neighborhood in 2002. I was pregnant with our first child, and we had a small budget but enough for a down payment in what was considered an "up-and-coming" neighborhood. We were moving from a similar neighborhood states away. Though I was excited for this new phase, the sting of saying goodbye to trusted friends, a church community, and a work team was palpable as I drove my new city's unfamiliar streets.

Our real estate agent had not shown homes in this part of the city before. Used to working in the suburbs, he was concerned he was steering a young couple new to town in the wrong direction. Though the landscape felt foreign and I was downright lonely, the neighborhood felt like the right place for us to land. Being with people who looked, sounded, lived, cooked, and spoke differently than we did was part of what we wanted—for us and for the baby about to arrive. Our neighborhood preference was part practical (close to Derek's new job, close-ish to his parents, and with a few affordable fixer-uppers still left) and part personal style (the pulse, texture, and color of the city felt most like home to us).

In some ways this was a homecoming for our family. We were moving onto the same street my husband's grandmother had lived on as a teenager in the 1920s, only a few blocks south of her house. She'd left after high school, never to return as a resident—until now, through the bloodline of her grandson and great-grandchild. It felt full circle and strangely comforting in the midst of change. But our new neighbors couldn't tell our family roots by sight. We simply looked like eager youngsters wanting to get some sweat equity from a fixer-upper house. Perhaps to move out to the suburbs once our kids hit school age, as many before us had.

When Derek's grandmother was a teenager, homes in our neighborhood were filled with Italian and Jewish immigrant families. Then came the wave of Latino families, some first-generation immigrants, others fifth. We were the faces of the latest change: young professionals who liked the proximity to downtown and to the freeway that led west to the ski slopes and east to the airport. Derek and I didn't need or want the neighborhood to change, but our very presence was contributing to the demographic shift.

Our new next-door neighbors were a family who had lived in their home for over a decade. A few steps ahead of us in life, they had three kids and were running from soccer practice to Mass up the street as busy parents do. Their English was speckled with Spanish, and the food they made was evidence of their Mexican and Puerto Rican heritage. As our relationship developed, humility was required on both sides. Conversations lingered over the fence. These impromptu meet-ups grew into kids playing together, meals, and later tears shared as our daily lives overlapped. Their welcoming spirit was a gift.

In any neighborhood in any part of the country, there are people moving in and out. In apartment buildings and cul-de-sacs and new developments, we live around people simply because they are next to us. Though intentional communities and neighborhoods exist, most of us sleep, eat, play, and pray right next to those who are different from us in many ways. We may choose a neighborhood or community knowing the general demographics, but unlike so many of those we are around in other spheres of our lives, we don't choose our specific neighbors. And they don't choose us. We happen to live side by side.

I find it interesting that given the apparently random placement of my actual neighbors, Jesus is clear that they are exactly who I must love—the strangers right in front of me (or next to me). It may feel as though we have nothing in common.

From life experience to stage of life to our taste in television, we could be as different as two humans come, yet it is a central tenet of my faith to love them to the same degree I love my very self. And when I approach my neighbor, I do it from my central worldview, one I have developed over time through my family of origin, cultural roots, racial experience, education, life experiences, personality, political tendencies, and faith. I believe things about the world for good reason, as do my neighbors for their good reasons. I can dig in my heels, get a little righteous, and defend my beliefs as if I'm defending my very life. But when I am defensive I have a difficult time being loving.

This is where a posture of humility comes in. We must love our neighbors from an understanding of who we are and who they are—and certainly who God is—in this world. The more I am aware of my worldview and where it comes from, the more I am able to learn from the person who experiences and looks at life differently than I do. This not only helps me better understand my neighbor; it also helps me better see God working in diverse ways in the world.

The Message describes Jesus's arrival on this earth as "the Word became flesh and blood, and moved into the neighborhood" (John 1:14). Jesus came to be with us. To walk our streets, eat our food, sleep in our homes. The one who crafted the solar system and breathes life into each one of us, who holds time in his hands, chose to come to this earth in the humblest way, the way we all have, through a flesh-and-blood mother. Don't get me wrong—my family and I were not under the impression that our new neighbors needed us like they need Jesus. Rather, we looked to Jesus as our model for being with people . . . *actually* with them.

His "moving into the neighborhood" indicated proximity is important.

The first directive in 2 Peter 1:5–9 is to add "goodness" or "good character" to our faith. As with most things of value in this life, the hard work of loving our actual neighbor begins in the secret places: our hearts and minds. Good character is an outer expression of our inner virtue. Self-examination is refining work and is not easy. In fact, I usually want to avoid anything that has the potential to make me uncomfortable. So examining and evaluating the gunk inside of my heart? I'll take a pass. Which is why I need to practice *holding a posture of humility*. It doesn't come naturally.

Standing with Good Posture

I've been working on my physical posture, my core strength, the last few years. As middle age hits, things tend toward the soft and droopy. Posture is the way we stand, hold our bodies. I often think of "good" or "bad" posture as standing up straight or slouching over. I have to do exercises aimed at strengthening my core because my posture is determined by how I carry my body's frame. If I don't strengthen my core, everything else is impacted.

The same is true of my posture toward the world. The way I approach situations, people, and God is related to how I hold myself. And this in turn impacts all areas of my relationships. It shapes my thoughts, words, body language, facial affect, tone of voice. When I get cut off by another car in a parking lot, I can let the "Who does he think he is?!" offense take root, or I can acknowledge with humility that I have no idea what is happening in the other driver's car or thoughts in that moment. From dealing with screaming kids to having a distracted mind, I've unknowingly cut off many strangers in my driving career. Remembering that helps me face the world with grace.

I attempt to hold a humble posture as I walk, talk, and interact. And it is strengthened with practice, because I'm not just humble once; I must enter humility over and over. Remembering I am neither the boss of the world nor the expert in everything helps me maintain this posture. The humble voices often get outshouted by the know-it-alls on both sides, outdebated by those with their crafted talking points, but God still calls us to this humble place. As worshipers of the all-knowing God, we admit we don't have all the answers, and we know our humanity limits our perspective. There is freedom in not being a know-it-all—and it's more inviting to our neighbors when we don't act like one.

Our family has been in our neighborhood for sixteen years; I'm now the seasoned neighbor. I've watched message boards fill up with threads debating the latest changes. Too many times newcomers have insisted on what they want changed, and old-timers have resisted while being offended that the way things have been are no longer good enough. The demolishing of single-story Victorian homes to build modern three-story towers. The use of school buildings by outside groups. The departure of the neighborhood bowling alley—a flash from the past—replaced with yet another natural-foods grocery store. When the online message boards go from sharing news to debating the latest change, conflict often stems from pride. If there is an element of "I know what's best for all of us" from either side of the issue, others naturally bristle.

When a person of humility steps in to redirect the conversation, usually through pointing toward the greater good, the tone changes. Working toward the common good becomes a search for common ground. This can be a shared end goal (improved schools, refurbished playground, lower crime) or a shared value (appreciation of local history, supporting small businesses, caring for elderly neighbors). When we are reminded of *what* we all want—that shared vision—we can often work through the questions of *how* with a little more grace and patience, even if our approaches are different. Humble people know their place in the world and use it as a framework for how they carry themselves.

However, this posture of humility is not something we can implement with the flip of a switch. It requires a practice of checking our hearts over and over again.

Heart Check: Pride or Humility?

The opposite of humility is pride. The world teaches us to be proud of our accomplishments, of our good character even, and yet we know as followers of Christ that we are sinners saved by grace. To be humble we must remember that we are not God, though we've been trying to prove we are since the Garden of Eden. Humility is remembering these truths:

God is God.

I am not God.

I am made in his image.

My neighbor is also made in his image.

I am a sinner saved by grace.

My neighbor is also a sinner saved by grace.

As I've been checking myself, considering my humility—or lack thereof—I've asked, *Who am I resisting as a neighbor? Who am I jumping to conclusions about?* I did a quick mental inventory to see where I could infuse some humility regarding those around me, and I drew a blank. Until God (I believe it was him) brought to mind one group of new neighbors I haven't been excited about.

In January 2014 Colorado made international news. Recreational marijuana shops were open for business. We were the first state in the country to make this move. We'd had medical marijuana dispensaries open already for a few years, but this latest development took many of us by surprise. As a community we'd voted for this change and collectively said yes to these shops, but I have resisted from the beginning. Our Denver neighborhood is snuggled next to downtown, right off the freeway that leads from the airport to our state's famous ski resorts, and seems to be the perfect location for tourists to stop on their way up for the "Mile High" experience.

You can claim I'm all kinds of hypocritical and double standardish because I have no problem walking into the neighborhood liquor store and buying a bottle of wine, but I've been fine with my double standard—and mad. Mad that every day I pass dispensaries in the less-than-one-mile drive between our house and the middle school. That my children can't help but have a normalized sense of this drug when they are surrounded by these shops and the lines outside them. That this normalization isn't helping anyone currently dealing with addiction. That outsiders—tourists and otherwise—have no problem driving into our hood to make a quick stop for a hit. That our state and our city were the butt of many late-night talk show jokes. That my neighbors have the right to smoke pot on the porch while my kids play in the yard, but my kids don't have the right to pot-free air.[1]

I could go on, but let's just say as the now old-timer in the hood, I have some feelings about the marijuana dispensaries moving in. Many of my neighbors don't agree with me (hello, we collectively voted for this). In fact, some of my friends frequent these businesses. So I'm also mad that this has put me in the position of neighborhood prude. I grumble, sometimes to people who feel safe (as in agree with me), and I make assumptions about young adults I meet who say, "Denver seemed like a cool place to move," thinking it's code for "People are cool with getting high here." All kinds of jumping to conclusions are going on from my end. Mostly I resent that these businesses have moved in.

So back to that good character, that posture of humility. In the same way God pressed those businesses on my heart, he reminded me of the people behind them. Sure, I'd thrown up some prayers in the last few years as I drove by my neighbors standing in line outside a dispensary. But I'd never prayed for the employees or owners or growers. And I knew my prayers needed to be agenda free. It would be easy for me to pray for them to see the light (read, agree with me), but that's not what God was asking. He was asking me to pray for them to experience him. To pray for people I didn't know. I could do that. And I could work on checking my assumptions about everyone involved in the industry. I could remember that God is bigger than my understanding of healthy living and could meet me and my neighbors through any means. It was a heart check, a humbling of my pride, that I needed.

When I remember everyone's proper place in this world, I can step out in humility. It is not thinking less of myself but recognizing I am not the center of creation. I am not in charge. I am not the standard by which the rest of the world should live. God has those responsibilities covered.

And when I remember that my neighbor is also made in God's image and has equal access to his grace, I can avoid acting as either rescuer or expert in how they are to live. There is freedom in offering love brother to brother, sister to sister, knowing we are on equal footing under God's overarching authority.

So as I work to add good character to my faith, I pray, asking God to keep me from stumbling on the pride that can come with such an aim. I pray that I will always remember who I am in relation to him and to the people right in front of me.

As Christians, we do not need to justify who we are; Jesus took care of that. We are loved and forgiven. When I'm tempted to advertise my accomplishments, qualifications, or résumés when talking with my neighbors, I try to remember that my need for validation has already been met. This means I do not need to look to my neighbors for approval. I can love free of an agenda to win anyone to my side. My job is to love God and love others.

"Therefore, as God's chosen people, holy and dearly loved, clothe yourselves with compassion, kindness, humility, gentleness and patience" (Col. 3:12). When I live loved, I am more likely to operate from genuine confidence as I reach out to my neighbors. Along with humility, compassion, and kindness, gentleness and patience are indicators to others that our love is more than a feeling; it is an attitude of care and service.

Heart Check: Motives and Assumptions

My eight-year-old daughter has recently been interested in helping with dinner. Our pre-dinner conversations go something like this:

> "Mommy, I want to help you."
> "Okay, can you set the table?"
> "No. I want to help you *cook*."
> "If you wanted to be helpful, you'd be willing to do what I need." (Yes, you can read into the snarky tone here. Motherhood has its limits.)
> "I *meeeaaant* I want to help you *cooook*."

This girl's motives revolve around practicing her new interest in the culinary arts. She wants to help me, but in a certain way, doing a certain activity.

Derek runs a ministry in Denver. Providence Network is a community of housing options for people coming off the city's streets. Their offices often get phone calls and emails from families in the community who want to serve a meal in one of their homes. Is one of their motives to meet the needs of the residents? Yes. Is one of their motives to expose their children to life under different circumstances? Often. Can this be tricky? Certainly. An innocent activity—making and serving dinner—can stem from various motivations. The result is we could unintentionally be countering our initial goal. If the people we are trying to serve sense our ulterior motives, the unintended consequence could be that they feel they are a means to an end—even if these ulterior motives are good, like wanting our children to appreciate how fortunate they are.

We all have motives when loving our neighbors. Many of them are altruistic: to become friends with our neighbors, to show care for them, to help them improve their quality of life, to offer them the gospel, or maybe just to be obedient to God's direction. No matter how well-meaning we are, our neighbors haven't necessarily signed up to be loved by us. Jesus does not command us to love our neighbors with an end in mind. He simply sends us out to do it. When we walk in humility, we are more aware of how our motives may be impacting our approach.

Questions to Ask Yourself When Checking Your Motives

Am I investing in the outcome or the process? Investing in the outcome means we expect some change on our neighbor's behalf. We fix a fence and expect it to hold up. We take cookies and would like them to be gobbled up. We send a text and want a response. But what if those outcomes don't happen? Do we feel disappointed, angry, hurt?

Instead, are we invested in the process? In loving? In expressing concern? In supporting and encouraging? Can we trust the process even if our neighbors don't respond or change in the way we would like?

Am I expecting something in return? A thank-you? A hug? A smile? Appreciation? Dialogue? Changed behavior? If so, are those fair expectations? Or are they about my needs getting met?

Some of my motives for loving my neighbors are not selfless. I want to be seen as the "good Christian" by others and by God. I want people to know I give back, I'm open-minded, I'm not one of those judgy Christians. I want our children to be exposed to people who are different or less fortunate. Or I feel guilty for how much we have (from finances to privilege) in comparison to others. These motives are about me and need to be addressed. I'm twisting what is intended to be about someone else and focusing it back on my needs. Just like my daughter, I want to help, but only

What am I willing to give up in order to love my neighbors well? Quiet? Money? Time? Physical comfort? Yard space? We are likely going to have to make sacrifices. Those sacrifices are often a clue to motivation.

Would I do it anonymously? Recognition can be motivating. Sometimes it's not appropriate to do something for a neighbor without letting them know who did it (we don't want to freak anyone out!). But if our answer to this question is no because we want credit from our neighbor or the larger community (this includes our social media friends), then we need a recalibration of our motives.

Will there be unintended consequences? Could a neighbor take our intentions to help the wrong way? Would they be correct—or even partially correct—if they did? Would there be unintended benefits from our plan? This question isn't meant to paralyze us from acting but to help us see blind spots where our good intentions can have a ripple effect we didn't consider.

if it's my way. *Holding a posture of humility* is the best way I know to combat this.

In the end it is impossible to be motive free. As followers of Jesus pursuing humility, we need to ask ourselves difficult questions and honestly examine why we're pursuing the efforts we are. We are responsible to know and understand our motives so we can enter these relationships with trust. As Eugene Cho says in his book *Overrated*, "Without being willing to explore our motives, to be deeply introspective, to give permission to trusted friends to ask the hard questions, how can we possibly act with honesty and integrity? How can we know that our care, generosity, advocacy, and pursuit of justice are not just a show?"[2]

When we talk about loving our neighbors, we are always talking about people—people who can be categorized into groups. Age, race, gender, profession, income, marital status, sexual orientation, nationality, and faith are a few. We may also have groups that we've created consciously or unconsciously: moms with kids at *that* preschool, people who live on *that* block, men who go to *that* church. We carry ideas about people who fit into these categories.

For years I've spoken to moms' groups. I've walked into those church basement meetings with assumptions about my audience: they are exhausted, they are overwhelmed, and they have lost a little of their identity in the mothering process. Often these assumptions are true of the majority of the room, but not always. Our biases can be based in reality and untrue at the same time. As long as we're making assumptions we will be living in the generalizations. It's not until we dive into individual relationships that we begin the work of understanding unique people and circumstances.

So I'm learning to assess my assumptions, to evaluate where I might have biases, and to ask questions like:

- Why do I believe this to be true of this person? Is it based on what I know of their circumstances? Of them individually? Of my own experiences?
- What other sources offer me insight into this person? Are they trustworthy?
- Would I think of or treat this person differently if _____ was different about them?

Checking my motives and assumptions helps me see if my actions are about my neighbor's needs or my own. *Holding a posture of humility* means, when possible, putting my focus on my neighbor.

Heart Check: Self-Focused or Other-Focused?

I recently interviewed author Gary Thomas on the topic of healthy relationships.[3] No surprise, humility came up. Gary said he taught his own daughter about humility this way: If a girl walks into a party, is fixated on how she looks and who she can stand next to so she doesn't appear the loner, and is generally worried what others are thinking of her, then her focus is on herself. However, if she walks into a party and sizes up the room to see who might need a friend, then her focus has shifted to the other partygoers and she is putting the needs of others above her own. As Rick Warren put it, "True humility is not thinking less of yourself; it is thinking of yourself less."[4]

If this is true, we first must become aware of how much we think of ourselves. We all do; it's human nature. Sarah Young suggests in her book *Jesus Always*, "Try to become aware of how much time you spend thinking about yourself. . . . If you're struggling with a self-centered idea that recurs again and again, try connecting to a favorite scripture or a brief prayer. This forms a bridge for your attention—away from yourself and toward [Jesus]. For example, praying 'I love You, Lord' can quickly direct your focus to [Jesus]."[5]

We can't be truly considering the other person if we are self-focused. When you interact with someone, do you wish to impress them? Wonder what they are thinking about you? Fixate on your own discomfort? Or do you consider what will make them most comfortable? How you can best give them your attention? How they are feeling in that moment? A great question to ask is, *What does this person need that I can uniquely offer?*

Love Can't Be Separated from Humility

The Bible is full of stories of fellow stumblers, those fighting against self-driven motives, trying to live out this posture of humility. We can see ourselves in the stories' characters, learn how they loved their actual neighbors, and then transfer the principles to our own circumstances. A story that appears in the Gospels of Matthew, Mark, and Luke gives us a glimpse into one group's active humility.

Jesus was teaching again, which meant the crowds had packed into the house where he was in order to see him (Matt. 9:1–8; Mark 2:1–12; Luke 5:17–26). A few men carried a paralyzed man up to the house to have Jesus heal him, but because of the throng of people they couldn't get through the door. So this band of men got creative. They climbed on the roof, hoisted the paralyzed man up there, made a hole in the roof tiles, and laid the man on a mat that they then lowered through the hole. They were successful. Jesus saw and then healed this man.

I've always assumed these industrious men were friends or relatives of the paralyzed man, because you must love someone dearly to go to such desperate measures on their behalf. Yet it doesn't say that in the text. Scripture gives no indication what these men's relationships were to the man they helped.

We do know, however, that the crowd was large and unwilling to move when this group showed up with someone who needed Jesus's healing. I'm assuming if this band of brothers was determined enough to climb on a roof and lower a grown man down from the ceiling, they had likely asked to go in the old-fashioned way, through the door, first. Based on their determination and unwillingness to drop their mission, I'm also guessing they weren't timid about their request to get through the crowd. Even so, the people in the crowd wouldn't make space, wouldn't squeeze in, so a sick man could get through.

When I read this story, it both stings and sings. How often do I—and the church as a whole—crowd around Jesus today? So sure that we must be the ones who need to hear him, who need the front-row seat, that we're unwilling to budge to make creative space for someone else? Yet this group of men figured out a way to bring their friend to Jesus despite the crowd's unwillingness to budge.

I can't help but wonder how they came to this plan. Did one of them have the crazy idea of, "Let's go through the roof!" Was there a worrier in the group, the one who constantly thought of every possible calamity? Was there one who had the brute strength to lift this paralytic up, or an engineer who figured out how to lower him down? We don't know about this group's decision-making process; we only know the end result: they went on the roof, took off some tiles, and let down their friend. I want to be more like them.

We can deduce that, unlike the large crowd pushing in to hear Jesus, this group collectively demonstrated humility. They placed the paralytic man's needs over their own comfort. They thought creatively, making a new plan that was different from how they originally approached the problem. And they stuck it out when things got difficult. If there was pride involved, which there likely was since we're talking about people, they were able to put it aside for the good of their neighbor. And the result? Jesus was so impressed by this group's bold belief, he healed the paralytic. He forgave him of his sins because these men (perhaps only acquaintances) demonstrated humble, pure faith. And as the healed man picked up his mat and walked out of the room (note that people were now making a path for him in the doorway), he was praising God.

What better example of humility do we as the church have than this band of brothers? Their desire to love their neighbor, combined with their faith in Jesus to heal him and their creative attempt to bring him to Jesus, made for a miracle we are talking about two millennia later. They embodied the famous definition of love we find in the thirteenth chapter of 1 Corinthians:

> Love is patient, love is kind. It does not envy, it does not boast, it is not proud. It does not dishonor others, it is not self-seeking, it is not easily angered, it keeps no record of

wrongs. Love does not delight in evil but rejoices with the truth. It always protects, always trusts, always hopes, always perseveres. (vv. 4–7)

The definition of love involves a humble spirit. Love and humility go hand in hand.

Adele Ahlberg Calhoun, author of *Spiritual Disciplines Handbook*, defines humility as "to become like Jesus in his willingness to choose the hidden way of love rather than the way of power."[6] And isn't that what we want? It is certainly what I want—to live the hidden way of love rather than the way of power. At least I think I do, until my instincts fight against that posture. Yet this definition of humility points me back to 1 Corinthians 13. Love does not boast. The way of power is controlling, demanding, and self-serving. The opposite of that is gentleness and other-serving. In fact, "the fruit of the Spirit is love, joy, peace, forbearance, kindness, goodness, faithfulness, gentleness and self-control" (Gal. 5:22–23). As we choose the hidden way of love, we encounter the Holy Spirit, and he gives us an inner strength from which this fruit grows. The more we can do to be in step with the Holy Spirit, the easier it will be for us to remain in this posture, and the more likely we are to find that good character we're hoping for.

A Modern-Day Foot Washing

When I think of what *holding a posture of humility* looks like, I think of my friend Kristin. As official greeter for the morning, she stood at the welcome desk for the children's program at her church. It was a typical busy Sunday of checking kids into classrooms, answering parents' questions, and passing out paperwork to new families. She noticed a mom walk through the door with four little boys attached to her, some hanging on to her clothes, others in her arms, and Kristin sensed, mom to mom, that this woman was tired. She greeted the mom as she plowed down the hall with the weight of four boys, helped her complete the required paperwork for first-time visitors, and walked with her from class to class to deposit the boys and make introductions to Sunday school teachers.

As they moved down the hall, Kristin had the sudden sense God wanted her to look down. She did and saw the woman's shoe was untied. The exhausted mom, her arms still full with a child and all of the bags that go with taking children places, looked down and saw what Kristin did: the shoelaces flapping long and free. Without a word, Kristin bent down to the floor and tied the woman's shoe. This mom couldn't muster the energy to do the necessary task, but Kristin could. And as she formed loops in the laces, tears started streaming down her new friend's face.

Kristin humbled herself by literally getting low in front of this stranger-turned-friend and caring for her feet. But the act was also an unintentional display of humility, saying, "No job is too small for me to let you know you are seen and loved." Shoe tying, at least of adult shoelaces, was not part of Kristin's job description. Not explicitly, anyway. Her stated job was to welcome parents and children. But she observed what this woman needed and didn't let pride, appearance, or position say she was too important for something so unpretentious. And this woman, who could witness her most basic needs getting met, felt seen and understood through this simple act.

Kristin doesn't have four boys close in age, but she does know what it's like to be at the end of herself. She knows what it is to walk into a new setting and hope for a friendly face. She knows what it is to receive an act of kindness, not because someone has to but because they want to. She wasn't able to offer this woman everything she needed, but she was able to meet a small, immediate need.

Kristin's posture of humility gave her eyes to see in order to respond. Seeing someone's need and being willing to meet it is standing in the space between despair and hope.

A CALL TO
Saturday Living

May we be people who pursue humility in the tension of life lived on earth with the promise of heaven. May we remember who God is and who we are in relationship to him, for when we do, we will not be confused about who is in charge. May we move away from our agendas for loving our neighbors and instead move toward listening to and following what God is asking of us.

Let us submit to the Holy Spirit so that we can offer our neighbors a taste of holy love in the midst of real, everyday circumstances, not because of our work, but just the opposite—because of his. *Holding a posture of humility* enables us to partner in the work God is already doing.

As we stand in this humility, may we remember we are here not to save our neighbors from their lives but to point them to hope. May we recognize that our neighbors offer us new insights into who God is, and may we look to see how they might be pointing us toward the hope of Sunday as well. When we honor our neighbors as image bearers, we reflect back who they are in God's larger story: his beloved.

This is Saturday living.

Questions for *Reflection*

1. What is your current posture when considering your neighbors? Are there any situations where pride is the voice rather than love?

2. Where could your motives be more about meeting your needs than your neighbors'?

3. In what areas might your personal biases keep you from seeing your neighbors as individuals?

4. How can you be creative in your responses to your neighbors' needs?

5. How can you live more in "the hidden way of love rather than the way of power"?

Practicing the *Practice*

- Offer an anonymous gift to a neighbor. Leave a note on their front door, sweep their sidewalk without them knowing, or quietly pay for the coffee of the person behind you in line.

- Look for the person in the meeting or party or school pickup area who is alone. Stand next to them. Maybe start a conversation, or maybe just nod and smile.

- Consider a specific individual or group you would like to better love. List your assumptions about this "neighbor." Examine the roots of these assumptions.
- Ask yourself if there are any unintended consequences that might come from your approach to love your neighbor.
- When interacting with a neighbor, ask yourself, *What does this person need that I can uniquely offer?*
- Ask God to redirect your thoughts to him. Come up with a prayer you can repeat when your thoughts become self-focused.

Scripture to *Digest*

Do nothing out of selfish ambition or vain conceit. Rather, in humility value others above yourselves, not looking to your own interests but each of you to the interests of the others. (Phil. 2:3–4)

2

Asking Questions to Learn

One who is afraid of asking questions is ashamed of learning.

Danish proverb

The heart of the discerning acquires knowledge,
for the ears of the wise seek it out.

Proverbs 18:15

In my early years of mothering I'd meet Jen at the park. The sandbox repeatedly became the place for me to listen as she talked with the newest stranger in our path. With just a few key questions, Jen would start a conversation and we would listen to a new friend's story about how she landed in Denver or her latest financial challenge. I used to say Jen could get a wall to talk, but really she has a way of getting people to open up. I'd sit back and listen as she worked her magic.

Another friend of mine, Krista, is known for how she makes people feel welcome and comfortable in her presence. I call her the mobile hostess because her welcome mat is with her no matter her location. She has an exceptional way of asking questions that draw others out, and soon they are sharing with vulnerability. Whether she's talking with my children whom she's known since birth or with strangers she meets for the first time, questions I wouldn't even think to craft flow right out of her. Once she asks them I'm immediately intrigued to hear the answers, because that's what good questions do: they take the conversation to interesting places.

We all likely know people who can get anyone to talk. They draw out stories and details with apparent ease. I've always thought that as extroverts, Jen and Krista were perfect matches for an introvert like me. I didn't have to do the awkward small talk but could stand next to them and listen in on the conversation, learning about my neighbors.

All of these years, I've blamed my introverted nature for my inability to strike up a conversation with someone new. However, I've realized I just don't know how to jump-start the dialogue. I don't have the art of drawing the other person out, of asking the right questions in a tone that is inviting rather than interrogating. Once a relationship (or even a conversation) is established—in full swing, if you will—my friends feel they can trust me, but how do I love those I casually bump up against so that they feel seen and valued? I believe questions are part of this puzzle, and if I want to love my actual neighbor, I need to develop this skill.

In 2 Peter 1 we are told to add to goodness, "knowledge," or "spiritual understanding." A way to add to our knowledge while *holding a posture of humility* is to ask questions with the intent to learn. My questions don't always reflect genuine curiosity. At times they sound more like statements. Other times they are attempts to direct the conversation so the other person says things they maybe didn't intend or want to disclose. I suspect that I've unknowingly offended people because I've overreached and jumped into what they consider private territory. This kind of question asking is the opposite of what I'm aiming for.

I want my questions to be an avenue through which my neighbors feel more cared for, not less. This is where the second aspect of this practice, to learn, is so important. It builds on the practice of *holding a posture of humility*. It recognizes that my neighbor is the expert on his or her own experiences and life. When I am in the position of learner, I'm acknowledging I don't have all of the answers. Relationships are by their nature a continual pursuit of understanding. Asking questions with the intent to learn helps us get there.

What Are We Getting At Anyway?

The goal in asking questions is to learn. It could be to learn someone's opinion, need, or experience. It could be to learn areas of common ground or places of difference. It could be to understand their daily life, family makeup, or work interests. It could be to gauge their opinions, understand their personal history, or know their worldview.

I suggest that our questions be aimed at drawing out the other person's story. Every person is larger than their politics, beliefs, or circumstances. The same defining song that sings through each of us is that we are image bearers, made in the image of our Creator. Because we as Christians know that hymn of personhood that resonates through our DNA, our starting place is one of common ground: we are God's children.

What I want to know about my neighbors is how this earthly, physical life has shaped them. Race, gender, and age impact someone's experience as they walk through the world. To better know who they are, I must ask questions that value their experiences. In his book *Ask More*, seasoned interviewer and journalism professor Frank Sesno says, "You don't need a degree to be a disciplined listener and an empathetic questioner. You just need to know who you are talking to and be able to imagine what the world looks like through their eyes."[1] My aim in asking my neighbors questions is to see the world through their eyes in order to love them well.

As I've observed great question askers, I've learned to consider the following when drawing out someone's story.

The depth of relationship. I shouldn't jump straight into "So tell me about your son's suicide" the first time I'm introduced to someone. Trust must be built. I may ask the checker at the grocery store if she has plans for dinner, which shows I see her as a real person and not just an extension of the register. The depth of question should reflect the depth of relationship.

The flow of conversation. I am not a reporter interviewing someone for the nightly news. My goal is to understand my neighbor's story so I can love them as well as possible. I try not to barrage people with question after question. I notice how they are responding. If they are expanding on their answers, they likely are enjoying where the questions are headed. If they're short in their responses, the conversation is likely entering territory that doesn't feel comfortable.

What's culturally appropriate. As Sesno points out, "Cultural sensitivities vary widely; one person's question may be another's insult. Some cultures defer to age and authority or view public questioning as inappropriate or disrespectful."[2] I can always start with, "Do you mind me asking . . . ?" Right there I am showing awareness that even asking the question itself may be difficult.

The Art of Asking Questions

So how do we get to the pulse of someone's story while honoring their privacy and respecting their space? The art of asking good questions is just that. Much goes into it, from how we state the words to our inflection, body language, and context. In order to ask questions to learn, we need to keep in mind what makes a good question.

Open-ended questions. These allow people to elaborate. Information-seeking questions that start with *who, what, when,* and *where* can make someone feel like they are being interviewed for a job or, worse, interrogated for a crime. Those that start with *how* or *why* get behind the story. They can get to the person's heart in the experience. For the purposes of learning about our neighbors, these are vital.

Follow-up questions. When we hear a detail that seems important to the story, ask about that. "How did you hear him say that?" "Why was that surprising?" "What were you thinking when you heard that news?" Statements can also fall in this category. "Tell me more about that." "I'm interested in this." "I'd love to know how you were feeling in that moment."

Open-Ended Questions That Can Be Starting Places

- What does your typical day look like?
- How did you decide to make this change?
- Who is your oldest friend? How did you meet?
- Who brings you joy?
- What brought you to this neighborhood?
- How did you hear about _____?
- Are there things you're looking forward to this week?
- What was your school experience?
- How did you two meet?
- How do you like to spend your Saturdays?
- What is your favorite thing to do with people who come to visit?
- How did you make _____?
- What made you laugh recently?
- What's your favorite activity on a cold day?

Clarifying what you've heard. Our minds unknowingly make connections when listening. Our assumptions and biases come into play here. Asking clarifying questions makes sure we understand the other person's intent and true meaning. "So if I'm understanding you . . ." "Do you mean . . . ?"

Later follow-up questions. Checking in with someone about something mentioned in an initial conversation shows we were listening. "How did that appointment go?" "Did you hear from your dad?" "Did the storm end up ruining your tomatoes?" Such questions show that we care about the details of the other person's life. (Tip: Set a reminder on your calendar or phone to follow up with someone about an important event. You may be the only person checking in on them about a given detail of their life.)

Be Prepared for Any Answer

If our intent is learning, we need to ask questions in a way that gives our neighbors permission to be honest. This means we must prepare ourselves for things that are difficult to hear either because of the pain, anger, or grief in our neighbor's answer, or because they create those emotions in us. Awareness of our own triggers helps us know what might make it difficult to respond in an empathetic way. Being aware of our nonverbal feedback helps as well. We want to be genuine in our responses, but at the same time we don't want to convey shock or horror if an answer isn't what we expected.

For a few years I acted as the Angel Tree coordinator at my church. As part of Prison Fellowship, Angel Tree connects local churches to families with children who have a parent in prison. I love the program because even though the church congregation supplies the gifts, the tags are labeled "From Mom" or "From Dad." Angel Tree provides a way for parents who likely feel isolated to send gifts to their children.

As the coordinator, I would call the child's guardian, let them know the child's mom or dad had signed up for the program in prison, and ask if it would be okay for the child to receive some Christmas gifts from that parent. Given the complicated nature of relationships, I needed to be prepared that the answer might be no. (It almost never was.) If it was yes, the guardian could request one clothing item and one toy for the child. I then would pass the requests on to our congregation, who would shop, wrap, and deliver the gifts. Most of the families were sibling groups. I was in a position to hear what all of the kids in the house needed.

I'm not sure why, but I was always surprised by a request for winter coats. As I made calls in early December in Colorado, it was hard to picture kids at that point in the year going to school without one. Maybe because I hear of coat drives at our school, I think every child in Colorado who needs a coat has access to one. Though I was curious, I didn't need to ask why the child didn't have a coat. I needed to know their size. I not only had to be prepared for any answer, I also needed to discern which questions were appropriate.

I remember one grandmother who requested jeans for her teenage grandsons. Nothing fancy. No designer preferences. Just blue jeans. I was surprised at the simplicity and unpretentiousness in the request. And then, picturing a thirteen-year-old boy trying to figure out life while being raised by a grandmother and needing some pants, I was overwhelmed with emotion. I was seeing just a sliver of reality in these young men's circumstances. This was not revolutionary. I have relationships with people who live in poverty. It was the specific answer to the specific question that took me aback and created an emotional response.

These unexpected answers are a gift because they indicate learning is happening. They are great places to insert follow-up questions so I can better understand the answers offered. As I remember that I am asking questions with the intent of learning, I can let go of making a point, being right, or impressing somebody else.

Questions are never asked in a vacuum. In order to avoid peppering a neighbor with inappropriate questions or to prevent bad timing, I can take into account various factors that will direct the conversation and the moment. I will likely be more prepared for the answers offered if I'm observing and aware of the context of the conversation.

Context Matters: Things to Consider When Asking Questions

When *asking questions to learn*, I've discovered it helps to pay attention to three things: nonverbal communication, setting, and cultural context.

Nonverbal Communication

"I don't think your face is conveying how you feel." Derek has reminded me many times that my nonverbal communication doesn't always match my intent. I tend to furrow my brow when I'm concentrating. This means I can appear angry or judgmental in conversation, when I'm actually just focused on what the person across the table is saying. Knowing my tendencies in nonverbal communication makes me more aware of them so I can adjust as needed.

Nonverbal communication can make a huge difference in how a question is received. Only 7 percent of what we say is conveyed through words, 38 percent through vocal element (tone),[3] and the remainder through nonverbal indicators like eye contact, body posture, and so on. Though these exact numbers are often disputed, it's generally agreed that body language and tone of voice matter in communication. So it seems we should pay attention to them. Leaning your body in toward the other person, making eye contact, even touching someone on the arm if appropriate, can convey care when asking a question. Uncrossing arms and legs gives a sense of openness, while crossed arms can project hostility. Facial expression will be determined in part by the question being asked, but generally smiling and relaxing the face offers a countenance that encourages conversation.

You've likely heard the expression, "People won't care how much you know until they know how much you care." The same can be true about what we say and how we say it. People won't care what you say (or ask) if they can't get past how you say it. With my husband I can request, "Please take out the trash" with the kindest voice inflection or with the opposite. My tone makes all the difference in what I communicate.

An exercise where you read a sentence aloud, alternating the emphasized word, demonstrates how the tone on a single word can change the meaning of the entire sentence. Try it here by reading the following sentences, placing emphasis on the italicized word:

I want you to take me to the doctor.
I *want* you to take me to the doctor.
I want *you* to take me to the doctor.
I want you *to* take me to the doctor.

58

I want you to *take* me to the doctor.

I want you to take *me* to the doctor.

I want you to take me *to* the doctor.

I want you to take me to *the* doctor.

I want you to take me to the *doctor*.

From stressing my desire to indicating I want to see a physician over other staff, the statement itself changes meaning with the emphasis. The same is true for questions. "Would *you* like to?" is a shade different than "Would you *like* to?"

How do we ensure our tone is warm rather than one that puts people on the defensive? It helps to breathe. When we are nervous or agitated, our body responds. We go into fight-or-flight mode, and our breath begins to shorten. When we start to feel our hearts race, we can take longer breaths. This can be done subtly—no need to start panting in the middle of a difficult conversation. It mostly requires attentiveness to breathing and intentionally slowing it down.

Speaking of slowing down, as we slow our speech and lower our voice, we can better control what comes out. We don't want to sound robotic, but we do want to be intentional about what we say and how we say it. For example, when I talk to a crying baby, my voice goes down in pitch and volume. It makes sense that all of us are more relaxed if yelling isn't involved.

Smiling also helps. It warms the voice. My senior year in college I worked in a call center outside of Seattle. Though callers couldn't see me, I was instructed to always smile while talking to the people on the other end of the phone because the warmth would come through in my voice. Granted, sometimes a grin is not appropriate given the topic at hand, but it's a good fallback when entering a fresh conversation.

Setting

Surroundings dictate what is possible and appropriate as far as conversations go. Sometimes I'm surprised that I am indeed in the right setting to dig deeper. I've had hour-long conversations while standing in my driveway, the kind that just kept going and going. It was not the place I would have predicted for a heart-opening talk, but I can usually read the room (or driveway) and know whether I should keep going.

Here are some questions I ask when evaluating whether a setting is an appropriate place to ask deeper questions.

Are we talking about private matters? If so, do I have enough privacy (background noise, space between us and others, etc.) to keep going down this road? Or do we need to move the conversation or pick up this topic at a later time when we know there will be increased privacy?

Is this a comfortable place for my neighbor, or does the setting alone make them nervous or uncomfortable? I worked for a few years with high school students outside of Portland, Oregon. They were all children of migrant farmworkers whose families had settled to work in the canneries year-round. Many of the parents had not attended much, if any, school. The school itself was an intimidating place for them. So I often would get in my Volkswagen Fox (yes, that was a car) and drive to the family's apartment or trailer to allow them to be more relaxed as we talked. (I also learned a lot from what I observed about a family's living situation.) Because I was in their spaces, they were not only more comfortable, but they also saw my willingness to make accommodations, which went a long way in those relationships.

Does the setting say, "We've been expecting you"? Hospitality is about making a place for our neighbors. Whether they are standing on the front porch, coming over for dinner, or spending the night, we want to create physical spaces where someone entering feels comfortable and welcome. This is not unique to our homes. Our offices, churches, businesses, and schools can give off the vibe that this is a place for people. Or not. Whether it's the language on signage or accessibility for those with limited mobility, I want my neighbor to know I have them in mind when they show up.

Cultural Context

Kendra and her friend Mary were taking a graduate-level class to teach English as a second language. Many of their classmates were international students getting training to take back to their home countries. When Kendra and Mary found out one of their Saudi classmates, Alanood, was expecting a baby, they shared in her joy. As the pregnancy progressed, Kendra and Mary defaulted to their typical celebration: they planned a surprise baby shower during class time. They picked a date and told everyone but the mother-to-be about their plan and what they should bring.

The day before the scheduled event, another Saudi woman in the class pulled Kendra aside and told her that in her culture it was considered bad luck to have a baby shower before the baby's arrival. What these American students meant as nothing but a generous and kind gesture unknowingly created a cultural clash. Kendra pictured the guest of honor's horror the next day when the roomful of international classmates and teachers surprised her with what they believed was a celebration.

Kendra decided to break the surprise and tell Alanood about their plan. Alanood understood the well-meaning intent and graciously said to go ahead as scheduled. In retrospect, had Kendra and Mary asked a few questions of their Saudi classmates, they would have chosen a post-birth date from the beginning and avoided the confusion.

In an interview with the American Psychological Association, David Matsumoto, a psychologist and nonverbal communication expert, said that there are certain facial expressions associated with particular emotions across cultures around the world.[4] However, the when and the how of expressing emotions is cultural. We may be able to tell our neighbor is happy because we recognize his laughter, but when he laughs may feel inappropriate or out of context to us because he is operating out of a cultural difference. The same is true for grief. We can recognize a sad expression but may be confused about how someone is expressing their grief. Cultural context is important as we interact with our neighbors because it explains things that otherwise may feel confusing given our own cultural lens. This also gets back to being prepared for any response.

How does all this talk about culture translate to asking questions? We must always be aware of our own cultural filter when entering conversations. This speaks to social norms; personality, which guides personal preferences; and our life experiences, which inform us about how the world works. All of these impact how we carry ourselves, our body language, and how we approach questions in the first place. Cultural context offers a larger sensitivity to how questions may be perceived and how they might inform us about our neighbor.

How we form our questions also needs to be filtered through a cultural lens. In his book *Leading with Cultural Intelligence*, David Livermore talks about indirect versus direct communication and how it can impact the process of asking questions. Direct communicators, who are comfortable asking and answering questions, may come off as blunt and often don't take other information into account. While indirect communicators often don't ask as many questions, they may take in lots of information through observations or general knowledge. Of course, all terms are relative. What may be considered overtly direct, even rude, by one person will be fine for another.[5]

What does that mean for us as we ask questions? We need to be culturally sensitive to what may be unintentionally offensive to our neighbor. When I spoke with the migrant workers, setting wasn't the only thing I needed to take into account. There were lots of dynamics playing out in those conversations. Here I was, a young white woman who had never done hard labor in her life, telling parents they must keep their able-bodied teenagers in school during hours when they could be working to help meet the family's basic needs. I needed to consider how they viewed my position in the school, my age, and the fact that I was a woman and childless. All of these factors impacted the types of questions I asked, whom in the group I directed my questions toward, and my word choice when asking.

I often asked questions to better understand the family's goals and needs: "What time in the afternoon does Bianca need to be home?" "What do you want her to get from being in school?" "How did you know to come to this town for work?" My conversations with mothers tended to have a better personal connection, but if the father or eldest son was in the room, the mother often deferred to them. I usually chose to follow her lead out of respect for their family system.

In Spanish there is a formal and an informal way to address someone. In many countries the formal is no longer used, but I always addressed the parents, most of whom were from rural Mexico where they still distinguish between the two, with the formal *you*. It was a cultural sign of respect. It was one small use of language that impacted how I communicated with them.

The dynamics of age, race, and gender, not to mention positions of perceived authority or lack of authority, are elements we likely can't change, but being aware of them helps us to treasure the people in front of us through respectful interactions.

Cultural context is also impacted by history and current events. From political movements to economic trends, larger forces outside of our neighbors' scope of control impact their experiences. *Asking questions to learn* can mean searching out reliable, trusted sources of information in order to understand the context of our neighbors' lives.

Asking Outside Sources

I have a friend at church who is from South Sudan. When she stands up on a Sunday morning and asks for prayers for her mother and siblings still in her home country, she often references the latest rise in conflict. I sit and listen, somewhat embarrassed I'm not up on the latest headlines in that part of the world. But I have access to information. Current news sources, history, and professionals in a given area can help paint a larger, nuanced picture. I can find answers to some of my questions from these outside sources. Being informed about the South Sudanese conflict is one way I can show this friend that she matters to me.

A decade ago my friend Ruth joined a group from her church to make an impact on the HIV/AIDS crisis on the other side of the world. She knew very little about HIV/AIDS, so she had to ask many questions about the health care system, how the disease works, and which interventions proved the most effective in reducing the spread. The people she met living with the disease were the most helpful in offering personal insights, but many other sources gave her information about public health and strategic approaches to treatment. From documentaries to books, she searched out sources of information that helped her understand the disease with more depth and honesty and determine how best to use her specific talents to love her neighbors in this area.

We always trust our neighbors to be the keepers of their stories. Every person is more than a trend, a statistic, or a movement. We can use outside information to help us understand context, but the person in front of us is always the primary source of their own experience. As responsible consumers we know that much of the information we receive from news sources comes with a slant. When we are surrounded by our self-created echo chambers, we don't always get an accurate picture of an issue. So in my journey of loving my actual neighbors, I consider how Scripture directs me to behave toward them, what the fruit of the Spirit looks like, and what it means to be a hope bearer in our interactions.

Often it is our neighbors and their stories that spark larger questions in us. We see disparities in the world, or our assumptions about life and people are challenged. We can turn to God with many of our larger questions. Asking him the hard questions is both a product of and a benefit to loving our neighbors. He is also a reliable source of information, so we can freely ask. In fact, I think he's waiting for us to approach him.

Asking Questions of God

I was crying so hard I couldn't breathe. I was a college student studying in Mexico, an easy thing to fit in my schedule since I was a Spanish major. My change-the-world, altruistic twenty-year-old self had signed up for a service-learning semester. I wanted to do good while I was there. When I arrived at the beginning of the semester, I was assigned with a few other female students to volunteer at a home for former street girls who ranged in age from four to fourteen. This was before the world of trafficking and the sex trade were talked about like they are today. I simply thought of this place as an orphanage, except the girls weren't up for adoption. It didn't occur to me that a four-year-old could be a prostitute. The program I was on should have offered me more context as I stepped into this situation, but it didn't. And I didn't know the right questions to ask of the staff in order to better understand the girls' situation.

One day I was playing with one of the younger girls. Our faces were a few feet apart and she was smiling, present. Suddenly her expression changed. Her eyes glazed into a stare, and it was as if she was transported somewhere else, somewhere inside herself. I had a new thought, a suspicion, that the disconnect between her inner life and her physical surroundings had deeper roots than her begging for food; it was the result of serious abuse. In a moment I had new clarity about the situation, and my heart broke wide for this girl and the world. I kept trying to play with her, engage her in the games that had made her laugh minutes earlier, but she was a different child.

I didn't cry until I walked out of the building at the end of my afternoon shift. Then the tears started, and by the time I'd walked the few blocks to my host home, I couldn't breathe. My earnest *Why?* to God came from a deep place. *Why this? Why these precious girls? Why not me?* If ever there was a gnashing of teeth on my part, it was then.

People have been asking questions to and about God from the beginning of time. When we live intertwined with people in different circumstances, belief systems, and realities, larger questions about life bubble up. *Why do I have this and they don't?* Or, *Why don't I have whatever they have?* From good fortune to health to material wealth, disparities become more visible and personal. The cruelty of the world becomes more tangible. We have questions about how God works and why he allows certain types of suffering and why certain people seem to carry a disproportionate load.

Living out of a posture of humility, we've already established we don't have all the answers. We can ask God to reveal them to us. From everything I can tell, God is comfortable with our questions. Injustice creates anger, and God is comfortable with that too. Throughout Scripture we read about people who questioned him. Entire groups came to Jesus with their questions, sometimes because they wanted to catch him saying something he shouldn't, and sometimes because they believed he had the answers. He welcomed their fears, doubts, and general misunderstandings, even their "gotcha" questions.

In John 11 we find Mary and Martha grieving the death of their brother, Lazarus. The sisters had sent word earlier for Jesus to come when Lazarus was sick, but Jesus never showed. Now, days later, he walks up to their house, and both women in different moments say, "Lord, if you had been here, my brother would not have died" (John 11:21, 32). Essentially, "In my greatest time of need, you didn't show up! Where were you?" Jesus was not afraid of their questions or even upset that they asked them. He met them there, even weeping with them in their grief. He shared their pain and gave reassurance that his love for them had not changed.

It's been twenty years since I asked God those questions of *Why?* that pulsed out of my heart in my Mexican bedroom. They are still part of the mystery of faith and of how God works in this world. This is not a faith with neat, tidy answers, but one that lives in the context of an often cruel and harsh world. Asking questions of God is part of my practice of *asking questions to learn*. I keep coming back to him because I trust him to love my neighbors and me. I trust his love for me, so I can trust him with my questions.

> Therefore, my beloved, as you have always obeyed, so now, not only as in my presence but much more in my absence, work out your own salvation with fear and trembling, for it is God who works in you, both to will and to work for his good pleasure. (Phil. 2:12–13 ESV)

This faith journey we are on is constantly working itself out. This is not earning or proving our salvation; rather, it is an ongoing process as the gospel, the good news of God's story in the world, changes us as we live in it. We must wrestle with these hard questions if we are to mature. And it is with a mature faith we are better prepared to love our actual neighbors.

A CALL TO
Saturday Living

May we be people who aren't afraid to show what we don't know. May our curiosity be genuine so that our neighbors see our desire to understand their experiences and who they are. May our questions demonstrate a love that counters the sound bites and reflexive responses so common in today's world. As my pastor, Steve, says, "Jesus walked toward people." *Asking questions to learn* is a way of walking toward people.

Let us express Christ's concern for our neighbors through this process. By asking questions we show that we are open to our neighbor's reality. That her opinions or his circumstances are not to be turned from, ignored, or pretended away, but to be seen as places where God already resides. As we ask questions we are learning more about what it means to be tethered to both the world and the hope that is Jesus.

May we approach God and our neighbors with honesty, always pursuing truth. Let us ask questions to learn about our neighbors and their experiences while simultaneously being sure of the hope our faith holds for today and the future, because the two are not mutually exclusive. When we stand in the reality of both, we are demonstrating that the good news of Emmanuel, God with us, is for our neighbors.

This is Saturday living.

Questions for *Reflection*

1. Who makes you feel comfortable in conversation? What does that person do that helps draw you out?

2. What do you need to be aware of (tone, body language, culture) when asking your neighbors questions?

3. How does setting impact you when you're in a conversation? What do you need to consider about setting when talking with your neighbors?

4. What reliable sources can help inform you about your neighbors?

5. Do interactions with your neighbors bring up larger questions about the world? Where might you take those questions?

Practicing the *Practice*

- Have a "how and why" dinner hour with the people you live with. Only allow questions that begin with those two words.

- Ask those who know you for feedback on your body language, tone, and facial expressions.

- Find reliable third-party sources to learn about your neighborhood's history or your neighbors' cultural context.

- In everyday interactions, ask questions you don't already have an answer to (and some you do).

- Create a welcoming space both inside and outside your living (or work or ministry) area to help your neighbors relax.
- Journal your questions for God.

Scripture to *Digest*

Teach me good discernment and knowledge, For I believe in Your commandments. (Ps. 119:66 NASB)

3

Being Quiet to Listen

Christians . . . so often think they must always con-
tribute something when they are in the company of
others, that this is the one service they have to render.
They forget that listening can be a greater service than
speaking.

Dietrich Bonhoeffer

If one gives an answer before he hears,
  it is his folly and shame.

Proverbs 18:13 ESV

I sat in the emergency exam room and didn't say anything. Our twenty-something babysitter, Concha, lay
on the exam table, tears flowing down her cheeks onto the
white crinkle paper covering the table. The tears both surprised me and didn't. By this point we knew she was going
to be okay. It turned out her collapse in our kitchen an hour

earlier was a simple fainting spell probably brought on by dehydration.

I was standing next to the stove when she said she didn't feel well, and then her eyes closed and she crumpled to the floor. My screaming into the phone at the 911 dispatcher is probably what brought her to. Once in the ER, I learned from Concha's conversation with the nurse that this wasn't her first fainting spell. It helped calm my nerves, if not hers, to hear that it wasn't anything serious.

Concha was the closest we had to an actual neighbor that year; she lived in our basement apartment. Because her friends were all at work that morning and her family lived states away, she didn't have anyone else to take her to the emergency room, so my husband and I rescheduled the morning so I could go with her. I took her to the hospital, and he stayed home with the kids since she'd been our planned childcare for the day.

Concha's tears were an emotional release. She felt alone. Though she was dear to us, the fact that I was the one with her emphasized that she didn't have anyone else to sit with her. I couldn't change the details of her situation—she was in the emergency room without insurance, her family unable to be there. I couldn't say anything that would convince her that her circumstances were different than they were. But I could sit with her. As she talked, I listened. I didn't need to say much to let her know I cared. I just needed to give her space to be heard.

It's easy to forget that our quiet presence is a gift of love. In an era of memes, posts, tweets, and hashtags, the front porch conversation is disappearing. The listening ear is now distracted. And worse, we feel the need to respond, to have an answer or an opinion. Our talking points are on the ready and we are prepared to use them. To prove we stand on the right side of anything. Yet what most of us want is to be understood. To be understood, we must be heard. For us to be heard, the person we are talking to must be quiet.

Our verses in 2 Peter 1 direct us to add to knowledge, "self-control" or "alert discipline." In other words, my response to new information (through *asking questions to learn*) is self-control and alert discipline. When loving my neighbors, I'm not to jump in with solutions, opinions, and comebacks. Instead, I hold my initial thoughts while I'm on alert to let the new information sink in. I step into that continued posture of humility and allow the understanding to sit for a bit. My impulse may be to quickly say things, to defend or retort, and then move on. But love is *being quiet to listen*.

What Listening Requires

Derek walked into the mudroom; he'd been outside a good forty-five minutes. I thought I'd seen him walk out the door with full trash bags in hand, so I'd assumed he'd be walking back through the same door two minutes later. But forty-five minutes later, here he came.

"Where were you?" I asked. I knew he had a to-do list longer than his day could handle.

"I don't want to be too busy for people." He'd run into our neighbor in the alley.

"What were you guys talking about?"

"Football." It is true my husband can talk football for a long time, but forty-five minutes' worth of football talk is long even for him.

Listening isn't always on our time frame or agenda; it requires us to put those things aside.

Our friends at Dry Bones Denver walk the streets with the goal of befriending the city's homeless youth, young people ranging in age from twelve to twenty-four who call themselves "street kids." There are about one thousand of them a night on Denver's streets. Much of what Dry Bones staff and volunteers do is listen, because listening builds acceptance. It says, "I can handle who you are and what you've been through. You aren't too much for me, and your story is something I hold tenderly." When someone is listening well, it conveys to the one speaking that they are the most important focus for the moment.

Here's what I've noticed about listening as I've embarked on this journey toward loving my neighbor.

Listening requires our time. We can't rush through the process with someone. In a world of nanosecond clicks, we may be tempted to skip to the conclusion, the punch line, the moral of the story. But listening is being with someone as long as they need to talk.

Listening requires our attention. We've all experienced someone looking over our shoulder at a party when we're having a conversation, seeing who else they might talk to. Eye contact, body language, and distraction-free living let the person know we're hearing what they're saying.

Listening requires focus. We really can't be hearing what the other person is saying if we're already thinking of our response. This is where I often flounder. It is birthed out of my desire to let someone know I am with them, hearing what they're saying. So instead of simply listening to their words and the feelings behind them, I'm distracted by my thoughts of what I could or should say. This does not help me listen well.

Listening requires quiet. I'm stating the obvious here. We can't listen and talk at the same time. We can't listen and defend. We can't listen and retort. We can't listen and interrupt. We must shut our mouths and give our neighbor the floor.

Getting quiet is sometimes the most difficult, disciplined step of listening. We really must practice being quiet when we're alone, before we can tackle it with the people right in front of us. It's settling in and waiting to hear, whether we are waiting to give the person in front of us more space to complete a thought before we jump in, or waiting to make space for the Holy Spirit to speak.

Even Jesus needed to set aside time for quiet so he could talk with God. "Very early in the morning, while it was still dark, Jesus got up, left the house and went off to a solitary place, where he prayed" (Mark 1:35). He was coming off a night of healing people and driving out demons. Word was getting out that he could do things. The whole town had come, bringing the people they cared about who needed Jesus's irreplaceable touch. This healing frenzy likely went well into the night. I imagine Jesus fighting to stay awake, offering his healing power as long as it was needed, but his body and his spirit needed quiet. So he did what many of us have done—he snuck away early in the morning. Even then the disciples tracked him down. "Everyone is looking for you!" they said (v. 37).

Quiet wasn't going to happen on its own. Jesus had to go find it. So do you and I.

How many times have I stepped into my bedroom, closed the doors, and cried because I've needed some space from my children and some . . . quiet? We often recognize our need for quiet when we've reached our max and are coming undone. For me, my angry words and tone are clues I need a break from the chaos that is my regular life. But if I made being quiet a priority before the unraveling, I may not need to seek it out of desperation as often. The harried moments would be less frequent because I'd built in the quiet.

In some ways I can relate to Jesus. As a mom I know how it feels when the crowd presses in, too many people touching me, climbing on me, even feeding from my body. I know how it is to be exhausted by the world's demands and the constant noise keeping me from being able to concentrate or sleep. And I know how it is to get up when it's still dark because nobody else is awake. To think Jesus understands this desperate, "all I want is a little quiet" feeling is comforting. Jesus's search for quiet time also indicates I need to make it happen. Because if God in the flesh needed some quiet, it must be essential.

But Jesus didn't sneak away just to be still; he also prayed. He needed to be in communication with God his Father. He told his disciples to keep things simple and quiet when praying:

> Here's what I want you to do: Find a quiet, secluded place so you won't be tempted to role-play before God. Just be there as simply and honestly as you can manage. The focus will shift from you to God, and you will begin to sense his grace. (Matt. 6:6 MSG)

When we are *being quiet to listen* in our prayer life, we can hear from God with more clarity. We want to hear from neighbors, and we most certainly want to hear God so we can co-labor with him in this treasuring-people business. Quiet doesn't just happen on its own. We need to be intentional about creating it so that we are more effective listeners.

Turning Off the Noise

"It was hard for me," Derek said. We were driving home from church, where we'd practiced stillness and quiet as a congregation during the service. "Three minutes of quiet and I realize how little I do it."

Just three minutes. And it highlighted, at least for these two Kuykendalls, how infrequently we practice this spiritual discipline. Sit with no sound. No reading. No music. No intake. We continued this exercise as a congregation every Sunday for a month, collectively practicing the practice, believing if we did it together it might feel a bit more natural to do it again at home alone. My three minutes that morning went something like this in my head: *What can I pull together for dinner? We have pasta and tomato sauce, but no meat. Hmm. Maybe we have frozen pizza. But on Sunday? Are the Broncos playing? Is it even football season? I shouldn't be thinking about this right now. Clear thoughts. . . . Did I pay for that kindergarten field trip? How do I know if the money made it to the teacher?* And on and on. Not exactly holy thoughts.

Silence as a spiritual practice is disciplined quiet. It is only here that we can hear God's whispers. Adele Calhoun defines it this way: "Silence offers a way of paying attention to the Spirit of God and what he brings to the surface of our souls."[1] Unlike prayer, silence is meant to be just that. I can get chatty in my prayers, even have an agenda for what needs to be said (read, what God needs to do), and there is little two-way conversation happening. But to sit in silence and clear my mind of all the random thoughts that float through—that requires focused discipline. And practice. Something I must do over and over because once is never enough.

The noise in our daily routines is more than just audible. As of 2017 the average person around the world will spend 135 minutes per day on social media.[2] That is more than two hours a day we are likely not talking, so technically we are quiet, yet we're bombarded with input that acts as inaudible noise. And these online interactions are limited in their scope. They can produce interesting conversations, but rarely do. Instead, we live in a series of back-and-forth position statements, "news" that is getting less and less informative and more opinion driven, and images of all things Pinterest-perfect. In many ways social media doesn't tether us to the real world.

As part of my search for quiet in my nine-month experiment to love my actual life (see my book *Loving My Actual Life*),[3] I took a social media fast for a month. I wanted to cut down on all of the virtual noise. In the process, I realized how often I reach for my phone or pull up Facebook on my computer screen without thinking about it. Phone scrolling is mental junk food—it fills the time, but not with substance or nutrients. It took a while for me to get used to not having that distraction, and I realized how it numbs the discomfort. I can use that virtual noise, whether a discussion on Twitter or an opinion piece I'm reading or a YouTube video of the latest lip dub, to avoid what needs to get done. Eliminating this virtual noise takes me to the same place the spiritual discipline of practicing silence does. It makes me more in tune with what is truly going on in my heart. This can only help as I work to love the people right in front of me.

The more comfortable we are with quiet in our alone time, the more comfortable we'll be with it in conversation. All this practice of quiet helps us when we are tempted to speak but should continue to listen.

Hold My Tongue (and My Fingers)

My fingers were rapid-fire on the keyboard. I couldn't believe how offensive her post was. She was talking about me—well, not by name, but she was talking about people who believe what I believe. And there was so much false information. I was going to show her and everyone reading this thread that she was wrong.

I stopped typing and stared at my words on the screen. They weren't being typed in love. They were born from a defensive place. They did not model the kind of care I wanted to receive. "Love my neighbor as myself" rattled in my head. I pushed the delete button and watched the cursor move backwards on my screen, erasing the heated words. Better to observe and listen. To be quiet in this online space where it's so much easier to say things that could be taken the wrong way. Nonverbals aren't available through our screens.

I can make almost any situation about me. Call it the ego or the self-centered nature of sin, but human nature moves toward self-protection. When I'm in conversation with someone about a subject on which we disagree, I have a need, almost a desperation, to show that I am right (and we all know desperation can get ugly quickly). In this practice of *being quiet to listen*, I need to push to the side all of these instincts to stand up and defend, to prove I am correct or at least somewhat smart or justified. "My dear brothers and sisters, take note of this: Everyone should be quick to listen, slow to speak and slow to become angry" (James 1:19). In a culture of increased outrage and extreme language, we are called to stand out as different. That begins with being slow to speak so we can be on alert.

My response in this moment when my defenses go up will build either a bridge or a wall. My hope in treasuring my neighbors, in honoring their value, is to build a bridge. Oh, this can be so hard, especially if the other person is indicating any kind of smug or less-than-humble attitude. Yet that posture of humility is what I am responsible for. I can only listen if I'm quiet. That is my job in this practice.

Hearing beyond Words

As I've worked to listen better, I've found that it's just as important to hear what isn't being said as what is. In *Blink: The Power of Thinking without Thinking*, Malcolm Gladwell talks about the power of observation:

> We can learn a lot more about what people think by observing their body language or facial expressions or looking at their bookshelves and the pictures on their walls than by asking them directly. . . . While people are very willing and very good at volunteering information explaining their actions, those explanations, particularly when it comes to the kinds of spontaneous opinions and decisions that arise out of the unconscious, aren't necessarily correct.[4]

I want to hear what my neighbors are telling me. As I said in the section "Nonverbal Communication" in chapter 2, only 7 percent of communication is conveyed through words, so I need to "hear" through my observations as well.

Here are some things I am learning to watch for as I listen so I may hear beyond the words.

Not answering the question. Perhaps someone doesn't understand what I'm asking. Or maybe they don't want to answer. If I think it's the first, I reword the question. However, if I suspect it's the second, I tuck that information away as part of my learning and let it drop. I am *asking questions to learn*, not to put the other person on the spot. If someone is avoiding a question, it's okay to move on.

Body language. Obviously the downcast eyes, sullen affect, and tears indicate that someone is not happy when they offer up the rote answer of "Fine" to the customary "How are you?" When body language doesn't match the words spoken, there is reason to pay attention.

Other observations. If someone is wearing a *Star Wars* T-shirt, riding a skateboard, or eating sushi, I am learning things about them. I can observe many things about my neighbors by listening with my other senses. Do they like to cook with curry? Plant wildflowers? Listen to merengue music? These could simply be matters of personal taste, but they could also go deeper into cultural roots, experiences, or circumstances.

Listening with all of our senses takes intentionality. Hearing our neighbors through observation also takes time. Just as our neighbors' first responses may be incomplete, so might our first impressions. That *Star Wars* T-shirt someone is wearing may indicate their love of all things Luke Skywalker, or it could simply mean they get hand-me-downs from their cousin. The more we are in relationship with someone and the more we are listening, the more we can integrate the information we receive to know how it's contributing to the whole picture.

When we actively listen, we can learn how to practically care for our neighbors. We get good information that can lead to action. This is true for us as individuals and also as communities of faith. Christians don't always have the reputation of asking questions and listening first before serving. We have been known to walk into situations or communities

What Active Listening Looks Like

Make eye contact. Look at the person's face while they are talking. Even if they are avoiding eye contact, you can send the message that you are giving them your attention.

Face them (and remember your face). Have your shoulders pointed toward the person, your arms uncrossed, and your face relaxed. Be aware of what your facial expression is telling the person talking.

Give physical cues. You can nod, laugh, or cry. Showing that a person's story stirs your emotions indicates you can relate and have empathy. If appropriate, touch them on the arm or back.

Allow for quiet. You don't have to respond the second someone is done talking. You can let the quiet hang between you for a minute. This allows room for them to continue in case they with a preconceived idea of what they need. We create entire mission programs based on partial information.

But not always. Many churches and parachurch ministries are intentional about listening first to avoid bulldozing their neighbors with misdirected love.

Listening with Intention

Discovery Church is nestled between the city of Denver and the college town of Boulder in the suburban community of Broomfield. Pastor Steve Cuss felt it was imperative that as

want to share more and shows you were listening rather than creating a response as they were talking.

Offer affirming statements. "That makes sense." "How surprising!" "You seem happy when you talk about her." Giving an occasional affirmation without interrupting indicates you're tracking with what they're saying.

Ask follow-up questions. "How did you feel when that happened?" "What did you do to respond?" Anything that expresses you want to know more establishes you were paying attention and care about what they're telling you.

Provide further follow-up. Follow-up questions can happen later too. "How did the interview go?" "How are you feeling about that conversation today?" These demonstrate that you haven't forgotten what the person shared and you are interested in the outcome.[5]

a relatively wealthy church, the congregation needed to intersect with the poor. But where? And how? He knew there were already people in the community who were serving these neighbors. He didn't want to duplicate what those service providers were already doing, and he certainly didn't want to compete with them. He wanted to know where the gaps were. What did the community's poor need that they didn't have access to through existing community services? Could Discovery Church help mend some of those gaps? Who could they ask? Who had already asked these questions and gotten answers?

Pastor Cuss knew most communities have some networking system for professionals providing social services. It didn't take long for him to find a monthly meeting of providers—a roundtable of social workers, case managers, police officers, and school administrators—to talk through service issues. It was a public meeting, so for months he attended. And listened. He could hear both the care these providers had for the community and their frustration in their personal limitations. Pastor Cuss let this group know that Discovery Church wanted to help meet their clients' needs. "If you have someone with a specific need you can't fill, send them to us," he said. "I can't promise we'll be able to meet every need, but if we can, we will."

Through listening first, the church was in essence serving and loving two sets of neighbors: the clients receiving the final services, and the city's social workers and case managers who often feel constrained by the parameters of their jobs. Often the latter don't have funds to purchase needed items like mattresses or cribs, or they are restricted by how they can use their funds. The church recognized these are hardworking people who are trying to do good for their communities. They shared a common goal: to care for their neighbors. So the church listened to what the social workers needed and helped them meet their shared goals.

From bikes to mattresses, Discovery Church has provided specific requests for specific neighbors. One spot in which the church has been especially helpful has been giving rides to appointments. The city's social workers can set up medical appointments, but they aren't allowed to transport clients. For the elderly, public transportation can be especially difficult. Walking to and from the bus stop, waiting in the summer heat or winter snow, is enough of a barrier to keep them home. Yet there is nothing stopping the church from giving rides to anyone, neighbor to neighbor, forging friendships in the process.

Word has gotten out that Discovery Church not only cares but also follows through with requests. Now, years later, someone else from the church attends those monthly meetings as a liaison and helps funnel needs to the congregants. Pastor Cuss continues to shepherd his congregation to love their neighbors by respectfully listening to what they need before jumping in with all of the answers.

Just as in our conversations with people, our conversations with God are often more one-sided than is good for us. We ask him for something or even ask a question, but then do not wait long enough to hear his response. We jump in with our agenda and plan. As we approach God with larger questions, we must trust the Holy Spirit in us to respond. But we must be disciplined enough to be quiet to hear the Spirit's response.

Even our prayer life requires *being quiet to listen* if we are to fully love our neighbors as God intends.

Prayer for Neighbors

We were stopped at an intersection. The person on the corner held a sign, words in marker on a piece of cardboard, asking for money. I made eye contact, gave a little smile, trying to be mindful of my affect. I didn't want to indicate fear but acceptance. Eye contact, after all, shows we are paying attention. I knew eye contact may also indicate willingness to offer some cash.

As a family we've decided we generally don't give money to panhandlers. Denver's homeless population is part of our

Ways to Incorporate Prayer for Your Neighbors

Whether on our own or in community, praying for our neighbors humbles our hearts and is an active yet discreet way to intervene on their behalf. This can be done alone or as a group, with your neighbors' knowledge or between you and the Holy One. Here are a few ways you can incorporate prayer on your neighbors' behalf.

Prayer walk. As you walk, ride your bike, or drive, pray for those who live in the spaces you are passing. A prayer walk can be around a designated spot, like school grounds or a park, or it can simply be your conversation with God as you go on a nightly walk through your neighborhood, asking for his kingdom to come and listening for his direction connected to those places.

Praying of Scripture. Words directly from God's Word can help us articulate prayers when we don't know where to begin.

family's mission. We give to our partners in this work of loving them. But we've decided cash to our neighbors is not our approach. So I kept my hands on the steering wheel, not reaching for my wallet. The man stepped toward me, and when I still didn't move, he stepped back, returning the small smile. I was quiet, no words said. And I listened. *Lord, help me know how best to respond.*

At that intersection I prayed. Sometimes my intersection prayers are silent, and sometimes, when my kids are with me,

Trust the Holy Spirit to guide you to passages as you pray for your neighbors. Listen to what God may be revealing to you about loving your neighbor through stories and words as you read and meditate.

Fixed-hour prayer. Set an alarm on your phone to pray at certain times throughout the day. Perhaps it's for a designated event, like your neighbors' safety during rush hour or the teachers during their lunch break. Or it can simply be a regular time to thank God and intercede for those around you.

Examen prayer. Examine your day and look for God's presence in it. Ask yourself two questions: *How did I love a neighbor well today? Where did I miss an opportunity?* Talk with God about your answers.

Intercessory prayer. Probably our most natural inclination is to pray for our neighbors by coming to God with requests on their behalf. From health to growth in all areas of their lives, we can talk to God about our shared heart for our neighbors.[6]

they are said out loud so we can come to God together. I offer prayers for protection and comfort. For God's provision and mercy. For friendship and for my neighbor to know they have not been forgotten. And sometimes I sit at the intersection and feel a prayer on my neighbor's behalf. That's when I don't ask God for anything; I simply consider the person and God at the same time. I listen for the Holy Spirit's prompting to direct my prayer. I step away from the request list and am mindful of God and his creation who stands just a few feet away outside my car window.

Prayer is our conversation with God. We can listen for his direction in the middle of a party or the middle of an intersection. Our neighbors will not know we are in this process unless we tell them. God knows what they truly need from us. It makes sense that we would go to him, ask him for something specific, and then listen for his response.

As we go about the challenging task of being quiet and listening in conversation with our neighbors, it's good to remember what the practice conveys. It offers respect and dignity to the person we are talking to, and it communicates that humility is our starting place. It takes the relationship to deeper places because it says, "You matter."

Listening Builds Trust

Derek and I started dating when we worked at the Dale House Project, a group home for teenagers aging out of the foster care system or completing a sentence with the Department of Corrections. These young people and their stories turned my understanding of the world upside down. Just as I'd started to ask *Why?* in college, I was being confronted right out of college with the very real consequences of kids not being protected by adults.

One young man's story gave a glimpse into the pain he'd lived through in less than two decades. He still looked more like a boy than a man. Like many teenagers, he had acne, was skinny, and wanted to be good at basketball. He wore a tight white tank top and Dickies shorts that were too big for him. Trying to fit in, he let his peers' fashion tastes impact his. Normal teenage stuff. I remember hearing details of his life before the Dale House. He'd seen his mom, a prostitute, get shot right in front of him a few years earlier. No one working at the Dale House was surprised he was now serving a sentence; the pattern of violence is too often replicated and the statistics were not in his favor. On one hand, he was a typical teenager wanting to fit in; on the other, he was carrying trauma too intense for me to fathom.

So much of our work there was about building trust, following through with things we said we'd do. This was new territory for many of the residents. If I promised to help someone do her laundry at the laundromat across the street, I needed to follow through because it was about so much more than laundry. It was about building a sense of security that I could be trusted. The same was true of listening. If I asked a question about someone's story, I held the details sacred, because this was about rewriting the narrative of what it means when adults say they are safe. It was precious ground we walked on, the paths of teenagers' hearts. We were showing them what it looked like to be treasured.

Of course, the more the kids shared, the more they knew we could handle the details of their stories. I'm not sure all of them understood the depth of their trauma—it was all they knew. But all of the kids understood that the world was not as it should be, that something was off. They could sense that. They just often believed they were the problem. So when I listened regardless of their anger, fear, tears, rage, and distance and kept coming back for more, I was building trust. I'm not under the impression that I was their healer; their wounds ran deep and I'm not God. But every minute I was quietly attentive, I reinforced what we were telling them with words: you matter. By listening and not showing shock at the details or mirroring their loud emotions, I could convey that my love—God's love for them through me—was more dependable than their pain. Our quiet responses are often our loudest.

Moving to Uncommon Ground

When we talk with our neighbors and are quiet to listen to their answers and observe the details of their lives, we find common ground. This is our initial touch point: we both are parents, we both are grateful for Fridays and the weekend ahead, we both like (or don't like) our neighbors' new fuchsia front door. We bond over these common places. We see each other's humanity in them.

But when we allow enough space for quiet, we also find what I call "uncommon ground." We get to what is dissimilar about us, which can begin to get us out of our comfort zones. What feels different catches our attention because it is less familiar, perhaps even intimidating. We can see these differences with more clarity when we are quiet enough to listen.

I have a friend who lives states away. We met years ago as we headed to the same weekend event. We sat next to each other in the shuttle van taking us from the airport to the retreat center and immediately connected. I found her to be funny (and even better from an ego perspective, she found me to be funny). We were both moms trying to figure out work, parenting, and marriage.

As retreat attendees often do, we promised to stay in touch when we said our goodbyes. As years passed and we had minor conversations about race, about her experience as a black woman, I didn't do a good job of asking questions and then *being quiet to listen*. Why? Likely because I didn't want to be uncomfortable with the reality of her answers. I didn't want to face the totality of her experience. I let my comfort dictate the depth of our relationship.

But I knew this was an area where I needed to do some listening. So when a few things sparked a conversation about race and she was willing to talk about her experience, I knew it was time to be quiet and listen. She was gracious to share. I was surprised that my tendency was to fight being quiet to listen. I found myself wanting to defend my understanding of her life. I wanted to explain that somehow I was not like other white women. That I thought about these things. That I put my kids in schools where they were not the racial majority on purpose. But that was pride sneaking in. Those thoughts and feelings were about me. If I wanted to love *her*, I needed to be quiet and listen. The spirit of humility had to be present—the questions and then the listening. The quiet.

One day I texted her, "I don't want to just live in the common ground. I want to know our uncommon ground too." Common ground is good. It's a starting place, a bonding place. It's where we intersect. We'd found those areas naturally and quickly. But that was where our relationship stopped because I wasn't willing to ask questions and then shut my mouth to listen. If we were to go deeper in our friendship, we needed to also explore the places where we didn't overlap.

To really understand and love our neighbor, we must be willing to tread into uncommon ground. The place that perhaps makes us squirm a bit because it is unfamiliar or straight-up uncomfortable. The space where we hold our tongue and let the other person speak. The only way into uncommon ground is through listening. And this is the soil of deeper connection. It is interesting, rich, sometimes uncomfortable territory. We are better neighbors when we step onto this ground.

A CALL TO Saturday Living

May we be people who offer the world and our neighbors a little bit of quiet to listen. In a culture and time where everyone is offering extreme responses, may we resist the temptation to offer the same. Rather, let us love the people right in front of us by believing that what they have to say is important and being on the edge of our seats when they speak. Whether we're actively listening with a neighbor or sitting in silence to hear God's direction, *being quiet to listen* demonstrates to both God and our neighbors that we want to love well.

Let us be people who build trust in this in-between Saturday space. As we listen bit by bit to our neighbors' stories, may we establish that we're more interested in learning about their experience than in offering our theology or arguing the next point. May we look beyond our common humanity (which is a great place to start) to see them as unique reflections of God's creation in this world.

May we accept and appreciate our neighbors' human nature and divine reflection at the same time. Let us listen well to show we aren't afraid of either the sin or the redemption in their stories. May we expect both because we know God's larger story, where it begins and where it ends. Let us listen to our neighbors without fear of their answers so that we might offer them a small glimpse of God's love and acceptance.

This is Saturday living.

Questions for *Reflection*

1. When has someone listened to you well? What did they do or not do that indicated you were getting their full attention?
2. How can you be a more active listener with your neighbors?
3. Where do you tend to make things about you? How can you flip that to focus on the other person?
4. How can you pray for your neighbors this week?
5. Where can you search out uncommon ground with your neighbors?

Practicing the *Practice*

- Watch people's conversations at a restaurant or coffee shop and see what you can deduce from body language alone.

- Wait before responding to someone verbally to give them space to say more.
- Replace social media time with quiet time.
- Check your motives when posting or commenting on social media. Is the tone conveying care for everyone who will be reading your words?
- Create a prayer of examen, considering your daily interactions with your neighbors.
- Practice active listening with people you casually encounter. Eye contact goes a long way.

Scripture to *Digest*

Set a guard over my mouth, LORD;
   keep watch over the door of my lips. (Ps. 141:3)

4

Standing in the Awkward

The will of God will not take us where the grace of God
cannot sustain us.

Billy Graham

A man of many companions may come to ruin,
but there is a friend who sticks closer than a
brother.

Proverbs 18:24 ESV

I sat in the classroom, wondering how to get some of the
warm spring air moving to create a semblance of a breeze.
Considering I didn't like pregnancy or excessive heat, I found
them to be a terrible combination. My bottom sat in (or rather
hung over) a child-sized seat, and I wasn't sure which was

thicker—the heavy air or the tension in the classroom. I'd applied to sit on a committee for our neighborhood elementary school. Members were selected by the school district to represent various constituent groups: current parents, teachers, staff members, the community at large, and the school district. I was one of two who represented the future parent. With a two-year-old at home and a baby on the way, I fit the description. I also fit the demographic change of the neighborhood. White. College educated. New parent. What would it take for me to send my child to this elementary school? What would make me stay rather than move or opt for a neighboring school like so many before me had? According to the test scores, the school was failing, but how else does a committee like this measure success?

It was Wednesday evening, our regular meeting time. A comment was made along the lines of, "This has been good enough for our kids. Why isn't it good enough for yours?" I was okay with the tension this question highlighted, because the tension was there whether it was articulated or not. I would rather examine it and talk about it than pretend it away. Honestly, all of these years later I don't know if that sentiment was worded so directly or if it was just made clear by the defensive tone and surrounding remarks. But I absorbed it because I knew it had truth to it. I also knew this was my first go as a parent, and though I hadn't been part of the solution before, I could be now. I wanted to justify the need for some changes, but I thought the numbers spoke for themselves. Many of us felt something had to change for *all* kids' sakes; no child deserved a failing school.

Let's just say Wednesday evenings in that classroom were hot in many ways for a few months.

Things can get awkward and uncomfortable when we stand with our neighbors. In fact, if they don't, we can wonder if we're truly living the call to love as Jesus did. If we start with *holding a posture of humility*, *asking questions to learn*, and *being quiet to listen*, there is a higher chance we will be comfortable in awkward situations. The parents and teachers who'd been in that school for years knew details the rest of us didn't. Those of us new to the proverbial table had some fresh perspective to offer. But all of us had to deal with some difficult realities if we were to make decisions that would benefit our neighborhood children. This meant treating one another with respect, perseverance, and honesty couched in grace. Second Peter 1:6 speaks to this when it tells us to "add . . . to self-control, perseverance" or "passionate patience." To look past the quick fixes and to hold the long view. To stand in the uncomfortable rather than run from it. To be willing to hang in there when conversations or circumstances get downright awkward, believing that won't always be the case, and even if it is, that loving our neighbors is worth the trouble.

Pursuing the Uncomfortable

The first few times we try something new, whether it's driving downtown or making eggs Benedict, it feels awkward, and we have to focus on what we're doing. But the more we practice, the less klutzy it becomes over time. Even the feeling of awkward can become something we get used to. The more we put ourselves in new, even uncomfortable, situations, the more likely we are to be okay with that feeling. We are then more willing to step into a new and different experience, expecting the familiar awkward.

For a number of years we had a neighbor (let's call her Betty) who would show up at her dad's apartment and stay a while. Sometimes Betty's stay lasted weeks, other times months, and then she'd be gone again. We'd know she was back because we would hear her standing in the front yard yelling, her deep, coarse voice directed at someone inside. I was never sure if her voice was raspy from the yelling or the smoking, or if it was just the way God made her. However, I was pretty sure some of her departures involved a prison stretch. There were months when she looked healthier than others. One Halloween she trick-or-treated at our house. No costume, just a knock on our front door and her hand held out. My children, already home from their annual outing, stared at her and then me as I gave her treats from our bowl.

On the surface, this neighbor and I didn't have a lot in common. Our common ground seemed to lie in the broad arenas: We are both women. We both have feelings and know what it is to have joy and grief. The experiences that led to those shared emotions were likely different. Though we were the same size physically, I found her intimidating. Maybe it was that I'd sometimes see her with a cut lip or a bruise on her face. There was no question the whole world would put their money on Betty if she and I were to brawl. I don't think this about many people, so the fact that I had this thought at all shows Betty was different from those in my typical circles.

The day we officially met, she came into our open garage where I was loading the car and asked if I had any money she could borrow. I introduced myself. I figured money sharers should know each other. (Side note: I did give her money that day, partly out of my own discomfort. That was the last time. I don't regret it, but had I thought it through ahead of time,

I maybe wouldn't have made the same decision.) From that day on Betty and I were friends. With every interaction, every wave, every yell across the street, every request for money, the relationship felt a teensy bit more natural. I got the sense that Betty was loyal and we were now her people, as she was always giving us a "Hey!" before we extended one. Betty was teaching me what it is to be a good neighbor.

One day I came out to my driveway to find the jogging stroller, with my two youngest girls inside, missing. I heard Betty yelling and looked across the street to see her attempting to right an upside-down stroller with the two girls strapped in, suspended in the air. The hand brake had given out, so the stroller had rolled down the driveway and across the street, then flipped over when it hit the curb. My girls were screaming and Betty's raspy voice was trying to both console them and call for me. "I wouldn't let nothing happen to our girls," she told me when I thanked her for rushing to their aid. That "our" did not go unnoticed.

Betty moved out when her dad died. I saw the moving van. She came over to tell me in a single sentence that her dad was gone and it was her turn to say goodbye. I stood in the driveway and held her while she sobbed, the smell of cigarette smoke her perfume. It didn't feel natural for me to hold her so close, and at the same time it did. I could genuinely tell her I was sorry for her pain and that I would miss her. I was and I have.

Had you told me years earlier that this would one day be the scene in my driveway, I'd have found it hard to believe. This unexpected friendship came because we were both willing to stand in the awkward. I'm sure there were a million ways Betty could point out to her friends why I was someone she couldn't relate to. From painting the brick on our house to driving twelve-year-olds to soccer games hours away, I gave her plenty of reasons to shake her head in disbelief and wonder why we did the things we did.

I'm grateful that I stood in my garage or on the sidewalk those first few encounters. That I didn't walk away even though there were parts of me that were squirming inside because I didn't know what the "right" response to my neighbor should be. That I asked God to cover my time and the space between our homes. That the occasional police activity informed me but didn't prevent me from knowing a small part of the depths of this fellow human made in God's image. This was years in the making and worth every part of awkward. I'm grateful Betty made so many of the first moves in our relationship. Her friendliness was a presence on our block that's irreplaceable. If Betty ever shows up again to say "Hey," we'll give hugs and celebrate a reunion with an unlikely friend.

As we stand in the awkward, we begin to move from acquaintance to something more. Friendship? Maybe. A connection person to person? Yes. In the awkward we validate each other's worth because we are willing to stay regardless of our discomfort. Jesus was comfortable making the established religious leaders uncomfortable. I don't think that was just for the sake of awkwardness but to highlight that his message to love our neighbors did not match what he saw the religious community living out. Jesus showed us that our desire to love our neighbors must supersede our desire to protect what is convenient and easy.

We don't have to go far in Scripture to look for awkward moments. Throughout the Bible God does not seem worried about people's comfort; if anything he seems to push us toward discomfort so we can depend on him with more intensity.

Jesus, God in the flesh, made many people uncomfortable. It seems fitting to look at how he handled the awkward.

Jesus and Awkward Moments

Jesus often created situations that made other people shift in discomfort. Much to the frustration of religious leaders, he ate dinner with tax collectors, talked with prostitutes, and claimed to have the power to save people. Awkward moments were what he was known for. In fact, I'd say he created awkward moments on purpose because he knew how uncomfortable it made the Pharisees, those church leaders who seemed to walk around with all of the answers. But I don't think he was simply trying to make some righteous men squirm; he also was putting others at ease and reminding them of their value.

Jesus had been traveling, it was the middle of the day, and he was hot and tired. He sat down by himself at the village well, hoping for some refreshment (see John 4). A woman from the village came to draw water from the well, and he asked her for a drink. It was awkward. Right there in that moment Jesus was breaking all kinds of rules, and she calls him out on it. "You're a Jew and I'm a Samaritan! What are you doing asking *me* for water?" Everyone knew this was taboo. Male/female, Jew/Samaritan—these were groups that didn't mix.

We keep reading and find out she was a woman with a reputation, and Jesus knew this. She'd had relationships with lots of men. Small town. Woman with a rep. We get the picture. She was likely at the well during the hottest part of the day because she wanted to avoid the crowds and the stares. In her attempt to avoid an awkward situation, she was faced with this bold man who was creating one. In this moment Jesus reveals his identity to the woman: he is the very Messiah she has been talking about and is able to offer her living water. The disciples joined the scene and dared not say anything (they were likely learning you didn't ask Jesus why he was breaking the social norms), but that didn't keep them from wondering why on earth Jesus was speaking to *this* woman.

Then she rushes into town, telling anyone who will listen about her conversation with Jesus. In a moment this woman goes from trying to hang in the noonday shadows, as invisible as possible, to running through the streets, bringing attention to herself in order to tell her neighbors about Jesus. She moved from avoiding the awkward to embracing it, because the news was too good not to share. In fact, many of her neighbors came to believe Jesus was who he said he was because of her! One awkward conversation moved her from town scandal to evangelist. Did some people still look down on her? Likely, yes. But did many thank her for her willingness to do something uncomfortable? Also yes.

What did this woman do that moved her out of the awkward and into intentional purpose? She had to harness her courage. When we get that urge to avoid a situation or conversation, when we want to run instead of stand, courage keeps us engaged with the people right in front of us. Courage keeps us *standing in the awkward*.

Courage Required

I tell my girls, "You must be afraid in order to be brave." To walk into an awkward situation and decide to stay there requires courage. But what are we afraid of? Perhaps it is looking foolish (that's awkward in an external way), or perhaps it's facing our own privilege in contrast to our neighbors' (also awkward, but sometimes more of a discomfort of the conscience). Either way, we must be willing to choose to stand in the awkward. The intentional choice takes courage.

Courage to feel. We can numb ourselves out of the awkward; in fact, many of us do every day with behaviors that range from the socially unacceptable (pornography and addiction) to the more socially acceptable (shopping and scrolling through Instagram). Either way, we are escaping our feelings. When we begin to feel uncomfortable yet choose to stay in the relationship, conversation, or circumstances, we are *standing in the awkward*.

Courage to question. We may not want to know the answers, so we ask with trepidation. But the knowing may help us better love our neighbors. This could be a questioning of systems, status quo, authority, and decisions. Or it could be questions of our neighbors that may challenge our own comfort because the answers require us to change in some way.

Courage to stay. The whole thing about *standing in the awkward* is that we aren't leaving. We are planted. This tells our neighbors, "You are more important to me than my own comfort. In fact, I'm willing to bring on more discomfort because I'm sticking around." That message alone can bind people together for a lifetime.

Courage to be honest. We may need to be honest with ourselves about what we've held true, our past and current motives, and what we've intentionally and unintentionally done that may have impacted our neighbors. This can hurt, or if we are sharing things with others, make us feel vulnerable. But God already knows it all. We are acknowledging what he already holds.

Courage to admit we are wrong. As we listen to our neighbors while holding that dear posture of humility, we must be willing to admit where we are wrong, where we simply have held to incorrect facts, clung to false assumptions, and defended untruth. This can be especially hard if we've dug our heels in and made a case for these wrong facts in the past. Humility gets us every time.

Courage to disagree. Are we willing to be in that awkward place after we've listened and find we disagree with our neighbors? Being in relationship doesn't mean agreement. We often mistake the two. We can openly or privately disagree. But it is okay to be with people who believe, live, and choose differently than we do. Jesus did it a lot.

Courage to act. A hug. A note. A committee. A phone call to a legislator. A running for office. Action can take many forms. Some are by their nature very public. Others may only be seen by a particular neighbor. And some are anonymous. If after asking questions and listening, we hear God's whisper or feel the Holy Spirit nudge us toward an action on our neighbor's behalf, it behooves us to obey.

Once we've decided on courage, we can be intentional about walking into situations we know will be difficult. Neighbors have all kinds of life circumstances come up. We may not know exactly how to respond to them. But if we've determined to act with courage and embraced the idea of *standing in the awkward*, we can walk into those circumstances knowing our presence is sometimes our best offering.

Showing Up

I stepped into the funeral parlor with the words *What am I doing here?* ringing in my head. It was a service for someone I barely knew, but my mother-in-law's words had been the stronger voice: "People remember weddings and funerals. Who comes and who doesn't." I want to be known as one who comes, who shows up.

I wasn't sure where to stand, how to greet the others already mingling in the lobby, who I should hug and who would find that gesture too forward. I stepped into the awkward, the tension, and reminded myself I came to support, to be present. This moment wasn't about me, and I could survive a dose of the ungraceful.

Often I've been part of a community, school, work team, or church where someone experiences a crisis or a loss and the group so desperately wants to help. But not knowing what to say or the fear of saying or doing the wrong thing debilitates us. The result? No one shows up. Yet awkward is better than alone.

This showing up in hard times, where there aren't always appropriate words or prescribed social gestures, can be called the ministry of presence. That sounds nice, doesn't it? It also sounds self-assured and smooth and calming, when often I don't feel like that at all. I am full of self-doubt, questioning whether I'm the right person to be there, whether they just wish I'd mind my own business. But that makes it about me.

In the foreword to Preston Yancey's book *Tables in the Wilderness*, Jefferson Bethke says, "I always find it interesting that the way our churches are usually set up we are always looking at the back of people's heads. But at a table, we are looking into their eyes. Their face. Their expressions. What a beautiful picture that God not only prepares a table for us, but he sits with us. He looks at us."[1] Looking across the table, or across the street or fence, can often make us feel uneasy. Seeing each other in pain, in the midst of mistakes, in circumstances that are unfortunate and sometimes preventable, can make us want to get up and leave. And yet I think we as the church are meant to face each other more in these difficult moments. We are living God's kingdom come when we don't avert our eyes but are willing to see each other's realities.

One of the things we can do when encountering an especially awkward moment is to name the tension: "This feels weird to me. Does it to you too?" This acknowledges the discomfort and also gives the other person permission to feel the awkward. If we're feeling weird about an encounter with our neighbor, there's a good chance they are too. Why not throw a little honesty, and maybe levity, into the mix? Being those who feel the uncomfortable yet don't leave is a great reputation for Jesus people to have.

When we practice *standing in the awkward*, our neighbors know we care about them more than we care about our own comfort. If we stay once the discomfort hits, the message is that much stronger.

Perseverance Required

"Everybody left when it got hard." It's a phrase we hear too often in every realm of life. From marriages to friendships to conversations, we can step out of the arena when we start to feel that itch of uneasiness. What does this tendency tell our neighbors about what it means to be a Christian? That we don't really care about them? That we aren't committed to our beliefs? As the church, we both excel and fail at perseverance with our neighbors. As Paul writes from jail, knowing his life is likely coming to an end, he tells his mentee Timothy to take the hard along with the good: "But *you*—keep your eye on what you're doing; accept the hard times along with the good; keep the Message alive; do a thorough job as God's servant" (2 Tim. 4:5 MSG). He is telling Timothy to stay focused on his assigned task and stick it out.

I've watched my husband live out this instruction in his work. In many circumstances when I would have declared "Too hard!" with a righteous dose of "At least I tried," he has persevered. Were I in his position, I would have seen the potential roadblocks and stopped, overwhelmed with the realities of the difficult work involved. But Derek often takes the long view, looking past the immediate issues to remember the larger purpose.

The time had come when Derek and the Providence Network staff and board knew they were ready to take on a new project, expand to a new home. The desire to house young adults specifically was something the ministry had been considering. So when Derek and Matt Wallace, director of Dry Bones Denver, connected, they felt collaborating on a house made sense. Providence Network provides transitional housing. Dry Bones builds relationships with Denver's street kids. Both are operating out of a belief that God has given every person undisputed value. They knew this portion of the homeless population had some unique needs and often weren't served by Denver's limited menu of housing options. "If we don't do it, who will?" they asked. Their obvious new assignment stared back at them.

So Derek started looking for just the right place, one that would feel like home and yet meet the unique needs of housing multiple unrelated people. He drove the streets of the city block by block, looking for a building that might be the

Questions to Ask When Persevering

Is the long-term goal still attainable? Can you still meet your original goal with the information you now have? If not, is there something new that is worth sticking it out for?

Is anyone at risk of getting hurt if I continue? When roadblocks come up in a situation or a relationship, it is good to evaluate if this is something worth pursuing. Relationships should not be abusive in any way, nor should you pursue persevering in abusive dynamics.

What are the unintended consequences of me sticking with this? Sometimes you must look at a situation from a different perspective and ask a different question to make sure you are not unintentionally causing harm. From finances to offering

perfect spot for these young adults to call home. And a home was found, a one-of-a-kind, stately mansion just south of downtown. Built in 1896, the carriage house still had marks from where the horses used to be stalled. It was full of potential. And the team's vision for what it could be was important in the months and years that followed.

The fundraising began, the negotiations were made, and the city permit was requested, disputed, and requested again. The realization that there was meth in the walls from years of flophouse living was just one unexpected interruption that needed to be addressed. The meth remediation alone took months and tens of thousands of unplanned dollars. And the respect, consider how sticking it out will impact those within arm's reach and those a few steps away.

Is the uncomfortable a place of growth? Do you want to quit because of your discomfort? Or will your obedience in persevering be a place where God can work not only through you but in you as well? Is the discomfort bringing up critical questions in you that need to be addressed?

What are the benefits of me sticking it out? What will persevering say to your neighbor about their worth? About your character? About who God is? What will happen if you stay? If you go?

Is God still calling me to it? This is likely the most crucial question. If yes, is he calling you to it in the same way you originally envisioned? Or are the roadblocks really redirections or places for you to think creatively?

whole time Derek kept his eye on what he was assigned to do and took the hard along with the good.

Then there were architectural designs, construction management, new costs, and hiring of staff. With each challenge Derek did "a thorough job as God's servant" so future residents would hear the message that God knows them and loves them. But with each challenge he also had to consider what God might be directing. Was the zoning dispute, disappointing fundraising event, or increased construction cost a sign that the project should be abandoned? Derek and his team prayed and felt the nudge to go ahead with the next step.

And the timeline? Well, it has been years in the making. The plans took some time, and then real-life setbacks got in the way. But the perseverance of so many on the team to keep working, keep fundraising, keep doing the thing right in front of them so they could house these young people, inspires me. Each person did the task in their assignment, often with an extra dose of creativity. The electricians did their task (until they walked off the job because they didn't want to work the week of Christmas), and the landscape architects did theirs. Even the man who sold the building wanted the property to have a legacy of healing and hope. He took a personal financial loss to sell to Providence Network rather than a corporate developer who would have demolished the home and rebuilt from the ground up.

It's easy to do the easy work. Stating the obvious once again, right? When we carry out the duties to treasure the people right in front of us, we must stick it out in order to "do a thorough job as God's servant." Whether sticking it out means having a ten-minute conversation with a neighbor across the alley who would love somebody's undivided attention as she talks about her cat's diabetes, or standing in front of the zoning board to create a new home for homeless young adults, it is all to love the neighbors right in front of us.

When issues come up, we are not to charge ahead simply for perseverance's sake. These are opportunities to reevaluate if indeed the task in front of us is still the assignment.

When Awkward Redeems

Dry Bones began hosting a weekly Monday evening coffee hour at a local coffee shop downtown. They paid for kids' coffees and gave them a chance to hang out in a place they'd usually just walk by. This gathering allowed kids to feel they were part of the normal public rather than the outsiders always looking in, literally and figuratively. As a staff person at Dry Bones, Robbie invited kids to join the fun. He approached a young man we'll call Tiger. (Most kids on the street have a street name and a given name.) Robbie's conversation with Tiger went something like this:

"You should come with us tomorrow night," Robbie said. "We'll buy you a coffee."

"Oh, I can't ever go to that place."

"Why?"

"They kicked me out once," Tiger confessed. "I spit on their window. The owner was so mad. I could never go back. He'd never let me back in."

Robbie pictured Tiger coiling up and letting out a big loogie on the coffee shop's front window, where it oozed down as other patrons looked through the now-not-so-clean glass. Then he pictured the coffee shop owner coming out with fists clenched and saying, "That's it. Don't come back. Ever."

Robbie could see how it would be awkward for Tiger to show up again. He also knew people can have second chances. Sometimes they just need a facilitator.

"Did you ever apologize?" Robbie asked.

Tiger shook his head.

"Would you be willing to?"

"Yeah, but he'll never let me back there. He was so mad."

So Robbie went to the coffee shop owner. He'd already been working with him, planning these evenings where they'd bring twenty unlikely patrons in, and asked if it would be okay if Tiger came and apologized. The owner said it would.

The next Monday evening Robbie and Tiger walked into the coffee shop. The uncomfortable factor was there—a mixture of regret, embarrassment, and general uncertainty on everyone's part about how the conversation was going to unfold. It lasted thirty seconds. There was no big sit-down, no mediator other than Robbie.

"I'm sorry I spit on your window," Tiger said.

"Okay, come in," the owner said. "Let's try again."

That was all. Not a lot of fanfare, a few awkward seconds, and coffee was ordered. There may have been a lingering awkwardness, but the initial discomfort was out of the way because all three were willing to go there. Willing to face the uncomfortable in order to move forward.

At first glance Tiger had thought, *Impossible.* The coffee shop owner may not have been keen on this reconciliation, but having a neutral, trusted third party in Robbie likely helped him reconsider. And Robbie was willing to stand in that difficult gap to be the temporary bridge. All three needed to stand in the awkward to have some reconciliation take place. This is movement in the right direction.

A CALL TO Saturday Living

Standing in the awkward is our new rallying cry as Jesus followers! May we be people who stand with our neighbors, no matter their experiences, joining God in the redemptive work he is about the business of doing. May we hang out in the in-between, in the uncomfortable, without turning from our neighbors' realities, where we aren't afraid of the pain, the grief, and the burdens our neighbors carry. Where we aren't afraid of their strengths either. Their culture, personalities, and even quirks offer us a richer life experience.

Let us plant ourselves firmly between two juxtaposed realities: the upside-down nature of a sin-torn world and the never-ending hope of God. *Standing in the awkward* is a foundation for highlighting this hope. Sticking it out when it's hard shows our neighbor a love that endures, and it shows that we aren't solely about meeting our own needs (we'd be outta there if that's all we cared about). Rather, our neighbors and their needs matter more than our comfort.

This is what we're meant for, my brothers and sisters in Christ: to stand in the uncomfortable, tethered to both the difficult realities of life here on earth and the hope of what is offered through Christ. Our neighbors will notice when we stay in this space, I promise.

This is Saturday living.

—— Questions for *Reflection* ——

1. When have you felt awkward when interacting with your neighbors?

2. How might you unknowingly be making other people uncomfortable?

3. When have you seen the value of perseverance? Where might you need to persevere on your neighbors' behalf?

4. How can you identify with the woman at the well in her response to Jesus? How might she offer a model for receiving living water?

5. Where do you see possibilities in potentially awkward situations?

Practicing the *Practice*

- Set a goal of putting yourself in awkward situations so you get comfortable being uncomfortable.
- Stay in conversations a little longer than you would initially. See where the awkward pauses might lead.
- Introduce yourself to a neighbor whose name you feel you should already know.
- Consider how Jesus might approach a given person or situation you find uncomfortable.
- Ask questions when you don't know something (especially if you think you should).
- Revise your plan to love your neighbor when roadblocks come up.

Scripture to *Digest*

Have I not commanded you? Be strong and courageous. Do not be frightened, and do not be dismayed, for the LORD your God is with you wherever you go. (Josh. 1:9 ESV)

5

Accepting What Is

I look at a person as an image bearer of a holy God and I am not in any way spooked by whatever worldly identity that happens to be attached to that image bearer.

Rosaria Butterfield

As iron sharpens iron,
   so one person sharpens another.

Proverbs 27:17

I sat across the meeting table from a man I'd met an hour earlier. We were part of a group discussion about ministry things, plans, and such. Two groups coming together to talk about the possibilities of collaborating. It felt a little like the two sides of the table were trying to impress each other, and in the context of that semi-posturing the man made a few self-deprecating comments that let me know there was a deep story there. He said he used to pastor a church. A number of crises hit, and life began to unravel. His pregnant teenage daughter was living with him and planned to release her baby for adoption.

As we stood up from the table to say our goodbyes, the group transitioned into smaller side conversations. I turned to him and asked about his daughter.

"I haven't given up on her," he said. "She may change the world yet."

"She already has," I answered. "She's having a baby."

I could tell by his smile he liked my response. I wasn't trying to be cute or clever. It was a genuine sentiment. As a mom I know my deepest contribution to the world is the four children I have birthed and continue to raise. It's easy for me to call that out in other women. I see world changers in the mothers all around me. This descriptor stems in part from what they do, caretaking and molding the newest generation. It's also who they are as image bearers, made in God's image. In that moment, my new acquaintance didn't need me to tell him the most sensational adoption story I'd ever heard, or to offer pregnancy advice for his daughter on bed rest. He didn't need me to try to fix anything for him (because, hello, I was in no position to do so relationally or practically). He needed me to validate her current contribution to the world, to be okay with what was true in that moment, and to see God in their circumstances.

There is something powerful about noticing the details of people's lives and stories and reflecting back to them how they echo God's larger story of redemption. This reflection conveys value and dignity and God's hand in calling every person into existence. No wonder 2 Peter tells us to add "godliness" or "reverent wonder" to our perseverance. To be godly is not to be godlike, but to understand who God is and live in obedience to and connection with him. *Accepting what is* means recognizing with "reverent wonder" the majesty and authority of God. This frees me to love my neighbors without the need to save them. It reminds me that the Holy Spirit does the convicting, so I can stand with my neighbors in love whether I agree with them or not. It feels like one big exhale.

Accepting what is also brings me closer to God as I search to see where he is already at work. If I am to partner with him in caring for my neighbor, to co-labor with the Holy Spirit, I must be in tune with what the Spirit is doing. That won't always be clear, but the more I watch for who is around me and sense where God is moving, the more likely I am to not only join him but also find co-laborers in love. The more time I spend in my own spiritual deepening, the more I'll be in tune with the Spirit's movement and in turn reflect that godliness Peter references.

How do we break down something like acceptance to practically implement it? How do we execute a sense of wonder for who God is and who he has created our neighbors to be, especially when it may be difficult to accept beliefs, opinions, behaviors, or circumstances we wish were different?

This begins with acknowledging that our agenda is not always God's. We must be willing to stop and recognize opportunities when they present themselves, knowing God uses interruptions of all kinds to bring us closer to him and his purposes here on earth.

Be Interruptible

I heard the lawn mower turn off, and I stepped onto the porch from the house. I found my then-boyfriend, Derek, talking to a young man I didn't recognize. Two things caught my attention: Derek's obvious excitement to see this young man, and the lawn mower stopped mid-row. My Type A personality kicked in, and I wondered if I would have felt the need to finish the job, finish that row, before turning off the mower to greet an unexpected friend.

Derek and I had been dating about six months. We were working and living at the Dale House Project. It was an emotionally taxing job as we tried to create a family-like environment for teenagers who had been raised on trauma. When I arrived to join the staff, Derek had already been there two years. Often kids who had graduated from the program would stop by, and Derek was a familiar face.

Turning off the lawn mower represented a trait in my future husband. One I liked. He made the young man in front of him the most important priority of that moment. He put more value on the relationship than on the task. Derek was the supervisor on duty that weekend. He had an extensive to-do list, which included getting the lawn cut. But what point is any of it if we aren't willing to be interrupted for the very people we are meant to love?

My surprise at Derek's reaction was steeped in the realization that this would not have been my natural response. Since that day, motherhood, the ultimate job in interruptions, has helped me improve in this area. I usually don't have the choice to live uninterrupted. As my children help me live out this practice, I get more comfortable with it and am more willing to put my agendas aside as real people in front of me have real needs.

What good is a program, a plan, or a schedule whose very intent is to love our neighbors, if I'm not willing to meet them in their actual circumstances? What drives my agendas to love those around me? What am I doing any of this for anyway?

The beginning of 1 Corinthians 13 says,

> If I speak in the tongues of men or of angels, but do not have love, I am only a resounding gong or a clanging cymbal. If I have the gift of prophecy and can fathom all mysteries and all knowledge, and if I have a faith that can move mountains, but do not have love, I am nothing. If I give all I possess to the poor and give over my body to hardship that I may boast, but do not have love, I gain nothing. (vv. 1–3)

In other words, the task can't trump the person. God's economy doesn't operate on to-do lists, spreadsheets, or blueprints. I love a good plan, but interruptions sometimes can bring me back to the true goal.

Jesus had a big mission, a strategic plan, an agenda, when he arrived on earth. He knew what he was about and where he was headed. But as he worked his larger plan, he was interrupted over and over. In fact, I get the feeling that disruptions were part of how he carried out his larger goal. Seeing how Jesus dealt with interruptions gives us a sense of what it means to be interruptible.

In the Gospels of Matthew, Mark, and Luke we find the same story. It catches our attention when three different writers make note of a single incident in their accounts of Jesus's life. Jairus, described by Mark as a synagogue leader (Mark 5:22), begs Jesus to come to his house to heal his daughter who has just died. This is an important guy, and Jesus has an important agenda to attend to: bring a dead girl back to life.

At this point in Jesus's life, crowds are congregating wherever he goes. He is pushing through the people when a woman touches his cloak. Not just any woman, but one who has been bleeding for years. She has visited all of the doctors with no success, has spent her money looking for a cure and found none, and has likely been ostracized for being "dirty" and untouchable. But Jesus stops. He interrupts his rush to the next miracle-making spot to attend to her real needs, and he heals her.

This story not only demonstrates Jesus's interruptible nature; it also demonstrates through the other characters the reverent wonder I am seeking. Both Jairus and the unnamed bleeding woman come to Jesus believing, or at least hoping, that he can meet their needs. In fact, Jesus tells the woman, "Take heart, daughter, . . . your faith has healed you" (Matt. 9:22). As he traveled on to Jairus's home, Jesus told the devastated father, "Don't be afraid. Just have faith" (Mark 5:36 NLT). I do not pretend to understand these answers. Many people of deep faith believe God can and will heal them, and he doesn't. So this isn't a formula for healing, but more a posture for us to take as we come to God with requests on our neighbors' behalf, knowing he wants to hear from us and believing he can change circumstances if he chooses.

I'm guessing not knowing exactly how this works is part of reverent wonder.

> "For my thoughts are not your thoughts,
>   neither are your ways my ways,"
>   declares the Lord.
> "As the heavens are higher than the earth,
>   so are my ways higher than your ways
>   and my thoughts than your thoughts."
>   (Isa. 55:8–9)

Part of *accepting what is* means knowing we do not understand all of who God is or how he works. It comes back to right-sizing our understanding of who we are in God's big world and accepting our neighbors where they are in their circumstances and processes. And in their emotions.

The Importance of Empathy

My friend Ashley and I were lamenting our mid-forties wrinkles. When you've been friends with someone since the years of smooth skin, you can laugh together when age shows up in places you never expected (even if you knew it was inevitable). "I guess I can just see how I've used my face," Ashley said, laughing. And it's true that one of her defining features is her vivid facial expressions. She shows a range of emotions, from her signature smile to her furrowed brow. As we're talking I can almost feel my emotions with more intensity as her expressions reflect them back to me.

Ashley spends much of her time sitting with other women in their pain. She listens and prays. She doesn't try to change how the person feels or thinks in that moment. She is empathetic. Empathy does not argue, trying to convince the other person what is an appropriate response. It doesn't try to help someone get over their present situation or move past the moment.

Empathy is an extension of *standing in the awkward*, because often other people's emotions make us uncomfortable. Anger, grief, and disappointment make us want to quickly move through the negative to get to the resolution. This is true not only of feelings but of circumstances as well. As a doer I want to fix things. But empathy sits and allows me to step into the other person's experience without judgment. This can be a learned skill, becoming more natural with repetition.

Empathy allows us to meet our neighbors where they are regardless of how we think they should be responding. Offering kindness is an extension of this acceptance and again demonstrates that we see our neighbors as image bearers who deserve to be treated with respect.

The Kindness Factor

Early on in my parenting I realized people could be categorized into two groups: those who smile at kids running through the grocery store and those who glare. I also realized I want to be in the first camp.

Though our paths crossed for just a minute, I still remember a grocery store stranger: her face, her dark hair, and most important—her smile. I was at the market a few blocks from our house and beginning to get used to the comments. We'd just had our fourth daughter, and apparently four kids of the same gender grabs people's attention.

"Are they all girls?" she asked. (In those early baby months, gender can be less than obvious.)

I nodded.

"Are they all yours? Four?"

Again, a nod. I was waiting for what felt like the inevitable, "Wow! You have your hands full!" or, "Will you keep going for a boy?" Comments that didn't exactly feel like affirmations of my growing family. Instead, she surprised me.

"That's so great!" she said. "We have four girls! It's the absolute best!"

Showing Empathy

No surprise, empathy is rooted in the practices we've already examined. We grow in our empathy as we grow in our understanding of our neighbor's situation and story. We are better able to relate to and reflect their emotions as we deepen our relationship. Here are some ways to apply empathy in conversation.

Verbalize what you've heard. Simply state back the feelings explicitly named ("You were angry") or insinuated ("It sounds like you were angry"). This helps the other person feel understood or clarifies misunderstandings or misinterpretations.

Affirm the other person's feelings. Letting people know their response was normal (whether appropriate or healthy or not) helps them feel safe. "That sounds like a normal response." "I can see why you would feel that way." "I'm not at all surprised." Intense emotions may be calmed if someone feels heard.

Be flexible in your responses. As emotions fluctuate, be prepared to meet the person where they go. If talking about anger leads to a place of deeper grief, or if tears turn to laughter, be okay with the change. Giving people freedom to have whatever feelings they need to is a priceless gift.

Don't mistake empathy for approval. We can get wound up in believing our affirmation of someone's experience means we approve of every decision, thought, or belief that went into it. Let that correlation go. Empathy identifies with the feelings; it doesn't mean endorsement of the behavior.

Her words pulled me out of my exhausted fog, and I focused in on her. I had a new interest in this woman. She was older than me by about twenty years—old enough to have raised some girls and survived. Her attention moved between the baby strapped to my chest and the toddler trying to wiggle out of the cart. While I was reeling from this new life of trying to keep four girls fed, clothed, and alive (bathing was optional for all of us at this point), she was ready to give a stranger a word of encouragement. And six years later I can still remember where in the grocery store I was standing when she said those words to me. When it felt like the world was skeptical of and overwhelmed by my inescapable reality, this woman celebrated it.

In fact, this same store was where I knew Frank. In those years of multiple babies, it was not unusual for me to cry in the checkout line. By the time I got to that point in the shopping trip, I was trying to push a cart weighed down with food for a family of six with one hand, while wrestling a kicking toddler with the other. I'd throw commands over my shoulder, hoping my other three shopping companions would obey and follow me without standing in anyone else's way or pulling anything else off the shelves. Always frazzled. Sometimes embarrassed. The tears would appear as I unloaded items from my cart to the belt and tried to keep my children's hands off the packets of gum perfectly located at their line of vision.

It was at this point in my routine that I would meet up with Frank the checker. If Frank was on duty I chose his lane for two reasons: he was fast, getting us out of there as quickly as possible, and he was a beam of sunshine. He usually greeted me with a "Hi, Mom" and then a compliment for one of my children. Unlike the shoppers, whose sideways glares were still sizzling on my back, Frank did his best to catch my kids doing something right. "They're so good," he'd say. Or, if he couldn't rightly give that particular compliment in that moment, "They're so beautiful." In the middle of my frustration and feelings of failure as a mom, Frank would include an affirmation for me: "You're doing a great job, Mom." Usually it was the only direct praise I'd hear that day. Because really, who else pulls out a "Good job, Mom"? I welcomed Frank's every time.

One day my oldest daughter pointed to a laminated placard taped to the back of the register, positioned for all shoppers to see. It was a picture of Frank, and my tears started as soon as I read the first few words. "It's with heavy hearts . . ." My mind stopped absorbing what I kept trying to read over and over: an explanation that Frank had died unexpectedly, and the details of the service.

The eye faucet was turned on full strength, and I couldn't stop. Tears ran down my cheeks as the twenty-something checker explained that Frank had a heart attack. That a group from the store went to the funeral that morning. That there had been a black cloud over the staff the first few days after they found out. No surprise. Frank was the life of the party.

I couldn't stop crying. Pushing my cart, my kids speechless at why their mom was behaving this way in public, I walked outside and transferred grocery bags to the stroller we would push two blocks home.

Why was I so sad? I knew nothing of Frank's life outside the store. I knew we shared a love of all things Italian. I had the sense he came from a big family but now lived in a quiet home. Most of our interactions were two minutes in length and included what I was making for dinner.

But we'd shared a few significant moments. Like when he had to cut my baby out of the seat in the cart because neither he nor I could get the buckle to work. "Well, she can't stay in there forever," he said. And with a dramatic flare that this mom appreciated, he called out for scissors and cut her free. And then there was the time he helped me with my bags during a blizzard. I can't remember if it was because the cart wouldn't move through the inches of snow that had dumped while I was in the store, or if it was during that stretch of "pregnant years" and I needed to be especially cautious in the slippery parking lot, but Frank carried my bags for me. I saw what looked like the shape of my minivan in the general area where I'd parked and slid the car's side door open. The teenage boy inside and I were both surprised. "You don't know which car is yours?" Frank asked. He was not willing to let the obvious go unnoticed.

None of those shared moments were life changing, so why could I not stop crying? Because Frank had handled my chaos well. He always welcomed my crew of criers, product grabbers, and shelf messer-uppers. He looked for the best in my kids and in me. And I realized I would miss him because that quality of loving people in their imperfect, chaotic messiness is so rare. I would miss him because of how he cared for me in just a few words and a few kind glances in our every encounter. If I could give the world some medicine these days, it would be a little more of Frank. Because the kindness of strangers goes a long way.

Welcoming Surprising Partners

Just as we experience a kinship with strangers, we can experience a mutual respect for people who view life differently than we do. When we find common ground, our connection to our neighbors strengthens. It can be surprising who might share a desired outcome, albeit for completely different reasons. Let's seize on that common goal and work together, rather than dismiss a potential comrade in action because we have different motivations. *Accepting what is* means accepting our common goals while allowing differences to remain. It means not dismissing the entire person or organization when we have some overlap of mission. If someone wants to love our neighbors with us, why not celebrate that?

My church, Celebration Community Church, has a nice-sized plot in the city. We have multiple buildings on a large piece of land: a field, a parking lot, and now a community farm. The neighborhood has grown up around the church's land, and by "grown up" I mean there are apartment buildings twelve stories tall that look down on this spot of green. On one side of the property is the beginning of blocks of concrete jungle with no park or playground to be found, which is partly why the church built a large play structure for neighbors to enjoy. Many of the residents of these apartments are immigrants from Eastern Europe and Africa. The adults sit in the shade of the office building's carport or at the church's picnic tables while their children play. The children of the church use the play structure on Sundays, but it is primarily a gift to the neighbors who use it every day.

A few years ago Celebration was approached by Urbiculture Community Farms about a large piece of the church's property, unused space between the parking lot and the curb. This group's mission was to create community farms in neighborhoods with limited access to healthy foods—"food deserts." Fresh produce is grown by volunteers with a pay-as-you-can model, making produce accessible to all neighbors. Urbiculture was scoping out potential sites in the church's neighborhood when they noticed the unused piece of the campus. For years the church had been planning on using that piece of land to expand the parking lot, a logistical need for a growing congregation and one that impacted neighbors in the high-density neighborhood. Parking is limited around the church campus, and the church allows the apartment dwellers to park in its lot on weekdays. A larger parking lot, like the play structure, seemed to be a good plan for both the church and its neighbors. But a few people on the facilities committee started to wonder if God had a different plan for the plot when this outside group unexpectedly contacted them.

Urbiculture had not worked with a church before; in fact, they were a little unsure about having an official partnership with one. The church had its own set of questions before jumping into an agreement with strangers and handing over a piece of its land for them to use. But the more they talked, the more both groups knew the community farm was something they could support. Not only would the space become useful, creating affordable, fresh produce for the neighborhood, but it would also be visually appealing, transforming a dirt patch into a well-tended garden with planting boxes, a picket fence, and an arbor. Regardless of whether neighbors took advantage of the garden's plots and produce, all of the apartments that faced the church's property would see a beautified space.

Urbiculture was looking for accessible, affordable garden space in the city. Celebration was looking for ways to use its resources to love its neighbors in the name of Christ. A church wasn't on the garden group's radar, nor was a community garden on the church's. When the two came together, decision makers for both had to adjust expectations and then amend the project's approach. When they did, they found an outcome both groups desired. This required an active and intentional acceptance of differences in order to accept commonalities as well. *Accepting what is* means we can mine for places of shared work while recognizing that differences exist.

When both groups took the thirty-thousand-foot perspective, motives and values didn't need to be nitpicked to death. There were differences in philosophy, but was God not at work as a result? Quite the contrary. God, the source of love and goodness in the world, is the source of good things, whether he gets the credit or not. We can see him at work and join him with unlikely partners, as long as our ethics are not compromised.

Collaborating likely means some letting go. *What about how they feel about X or their policy on Y?* you might be asking. We may have some issues that are a litmus test for us, those things we hold so dearly that we can't step over them. But perhaps we need to hold them a little less tightly if we are working on something that has nothing to do with that particular issue. Disagreeing with our neighbor on gun control or abortion or gay marriage or peanut butter vs. almond butter or anything else is to be expected. We likely aren't going to find many people (or any, for that matter) who agree with us on every detail of every issue, so maybe it's time to let go of that expectation.

It's easy for us to make a quick assessment about whether we want to be associated with a given person or group. Remember, potential collaborators are asking the same questions about us. Are we exuding the kind of love we want to be

Questions to Ask When Collaborating

Whether you are working with others on your block to support an elderly neighbor or your church is working with the police department to offer teddy bears to kids at crime scenes, we can partner with unexpected allies. Here are some questions to consider when joining forces with others to love your neighbors.

Do I believe in the work at hand? Collecting diapers? Yes. Making meals? Yes. Sending notes to prisoners? Of course. There are so many things we as the church can enthusiastically say yes to. Let's find those and link arms with others as we do them! We want to be people known for stepping into the "yes" rather than the ones always giving the "no."

Will this work strengthen relationships? We want to build relationships with our neighbors. When we are collaborating with

known for? Are we partners who have a posture of humility, ask questions, listen, and are willing to stand in the awkward? Do we exude reverent wonder, amazed at God's creation and how he is gifting our neighbors to do great things in the world? Before we can work with our neighbors, they must want to work with us.

Let us not forget that Jesus kept surprising company. Surprising to the religious leaders of the time, that is. They were not expecting fishermen (uneducated worker dudes who probably didn't smell so good) to be his go-to guys, or a tax collector (known for corruption and working for the state) others to care for those right in front of us, we get a twofold benefit: we love those we are serving and those we are serving alongside. Sometimes we have the greatest impact on those we are serving alongside.

Will it keep me from doing what God has called me to? Does it deplete the resources (time, energy, money) that are designated for what we are called to as a family, small group, or church? Would this work, project, or collaboration keep us from our larger mission in the world? When we are feeling scarce in resources, there may be another creative way that would allow us to do this work with unlikely partners.

Will I be asked to do anything that goes against my moral framework? If the answer to this is yes, we can gracefully bow out. Remember, being associated with someone does not make us absorb their beliefs. Awkward and stretching are okay. Feeling compelled to go against our moral code is not.

to be Jesus's requested dinner host, or women to be his ambassadors (Jesus first appeared to Mary Magdalene after the resurrection and commissioned her to go and tell what she had seen). Had the church leaders been looking at résumés, statements of belief, and past accomplishments to determine God's first army of believers, they would not have come up with this crew. But Jesus did. His choice of companions underscores that the good work to be done, his good work, is sometimes accomplished by unexpected hands. What unexpected hands around us are already loving our neighbors? Maybe it's time to join them.

Often potential partners bring skills and expertise we do not have. They may also have connections, manpower, financial resources, knowledge, and relationships. Though we may try to be everything to everyone, we can't be. Friends in the journey, partners in the work, help fill in the gaps. Or, as Steve Cuss's church (mentioned in chapter 3) does so well, we offer to fill in others' service gaps. Part of appreciating the assets that surprising partners bring to the work of loving our neighbors is recognizing our own limitations. Whether as an organization or an individual, *accepting what is* means seeing our limitations with stronger clarity.

Accepting My Limitations

The practice of *accepting what is* involves accepting our real constraints. We must acknowledge our own circumstances, physical constraints, and resources and remember we are bound by our limitations. We can only do so much for our neighbors—God is the only one who can meet all of their needs. Remembering this truth is easier for some of us than for others. As we discern the best ways to show love to our neighbors, we take into account our limitations and trust God with all that we cannot do. This means stewarding the gifts he has given us while recognizing they have limits.

The opportunities to love every person in front of us can feel daunting, and the idea of acting on all of them can sound exhausting, impossible even. Readers of my previous books know that the principle "Do what only you can do" has helped ᵗᵍe my responsibilities and relationships as I walk ₃. It not only encourages me to accept what .onally focuses my efforts on where I am most needed and effective. *Only I* can be Derek's wife and these four girls' mom. *Only I* can be my mother's daughter, and *only I* can fulfill this particular book contract. This filter helps me discern between what I *can* do and what I *must* do. I am not meant to make a meal for every family at school who's going through something difficult, but perhaps I can for the one within arm's reach. I can't volunteer for every cause and every goal, so I must ask God, *Where? When? With whom?* And then do the work diligently and to completion.

The Serenity Prayer, written and used by theologian Reinhold Niebuhr, is familiar to many of us:

> God, grant me the serenity to accept the things I
> cannot change,
> Courage to change the things I can,
> And wisdom to know the difference.

Now adopted by recovery groups like AA, this prayer reminds us that we have control over some parts of our lives while many of the details of the day to day are out of our control. The same is true when it comes to loving our neighbors. From attempted conversation to offers to help, we can only control our behaviors and responses and then trust God is at work in the unseen places.

As we look at what we can't change, at "what is," it's important to note that Jesus says, "Love your neighbor as yourself," or, as *The Message* phrases it, "Love others as well as you love yourself" (Mark 12:31). I often skip over the "as yourself" part. I just see the command to love others. I don't ask, *How am I doing at loving myself these days?* Probably because I don't want to face my own limitations. But if I'm not doing a good job caring for myself, I won't have very high standards for how to love others.

In some ways the idea of loving myself seems to go against the message of the church to "die to self." In fact, Jesus says to his disciples,

> Whoever wants to be my disciple must deny themselves and take up their cross and follow me. For whoever wants to save their life will lose it, but whoever loses their life for me will find it. (Matt. 16:24–25)

We are most certainly called to live beyond our desires, our comforts, our wishes, and to replace them with what God asks of us. I would argue that this is exactly what we are doing here in our pursuit to live out God's often uncomfortable command to love our neighbor. In order to fulfill that command well, we must offer our healthiest selves.

Caring for ourselves does not mean indulgence. Most of us can discern between needs and wants. The problem is, we often don't. Perhaps the first step is to ask God to reveal what we truly need in order to best love those around us. To ask the Holy Spirit to be the discerner, the refiner, as we dig into the practical applications of self-care, so we are living out of health but not unnecessary excess.

From there we can experience wonder at how God has made us—our bodies (hello, amazing!), our minds (we bring unique connections to everything we learn), our emotions (to feel is to know a part of God's heart), and our souls (there is something core that lasts). As we recognize our limitations, we are holding that reverent wonder. Much like *holding a posture of humility*, by accepting the boundaries of our energy, abilities, and control, we are recognizing our real limitations and where God is the only one able. This too is *accepting what is*.

When I distinguish between needs and wants, I am able to set up good habits that allow me to be of sound body, mind, and soul. These habits include

regular exercise

a balanced diet

sufficient sleep

healthy relationships

creative outlets

meaningful work

prayer and meditation

Scripture reading

worship

These healthy habits of caring for my body, mind, and soul prepare me to love my neighbors out of a place of personal thriving. If I've learned anything about myself in the last decade, it's that I don't operate at my best on little sleep. I am quicker to lose my patience and less likely to tackle what's right in front of me with grace if I'm operating on depleted reserves. So the more I do to care for my soul, mind, and body, the healthier I am and the more energy I am able to give to others.

It is a gift to have a body that holds our soul here on earth, with a heart that beats and air that moves through our lungs. It's a gift to be able to come to God with our prayers. It's a gift to do the things that give us joy. It's a gift to have opportunities to love our neighbors. We live an incarnational life on purpose. God designed it that way. By our very design we have limitations. We can fight them or accept them.

A CALL TO
Saturday Living

May we be people who embrace the neighbors right in front of us without agendas or expectations but with a reception that speaks love. May we accept what is, thereby showing our neighbors that we love them today, right now, as they are. At the same time, may we acknowledge our own limitations and remember our human constraints, allowing God to ultimately meet our neighbors' needs. May we search for places of unity with our neighbors and when possible accept, even celebrate, differences.

Let us be people who notice—noticing who is around us, what they might need, whom they might love with us, and where God may already be working. Once we've noticed, we can extend this love, grateful that we are placed here, in our actual community, at this point in history, to reflect God's love in a unique and appointed way.

Standing in the in-between is acknowledging the reality of this world while continuing to point to the reality of hope. This is the larger "what is" of the world. We don't need to be anxious about the dichotomy, because both are simultaneously true. We get to stand with our neighbors in this truth during a unique time in history. Pretty incredible.

This is Saturday living.

Questions for *Reflection*

1. How well do you handle being interrupted? What can you do to make yourself more available to God's purposes aside from your own agenda?

2. Who are you uniquely positioned to encourage this week?

3. Where might you and a neighbor have a different motive but a common desired outcome? How can you work on partnering with this neighbor for your shared goal? Who are some unexpected people you can join in this work?

4. How are you doing at accepting your limitations? Where can you find wonder in how God has made you?

5. What or who might God want you to notice with new eyes?

Practicing the *Practice*

- Stop and pay attention to the people you're serving. Let them interrupt you.

- When you think something nice about a stranger, tell them.

- Find someone who is already loving your neighbors and ask if you can help them in their efforts.

- Listen to someone's story and reflect back the feelings you hear.

- Incorporate one type of self-care activity in your daily schedule.

- Pray the Serenity Prayer.

Scripture to *Digest*

For I am sure that neither death nor life, nor angels nor rulers, nor things present nor things to come, nor powers, nor height nor depth, nor anything else in all creation, will be able to separate us from the love of God in Christ Jesus our Lord. (Rom. 8:38–39 ESV)

6

Lightening Up

A good laugh heals a lot of hurts.
Madeleine L'Engle

A miserable heart means a miserable life;
a cheerful heart fills the day with song.
Proverbs 15:15 MSG

It had been a long day at the water park, so when it was time to go, we were ready. We didn't even change out of our wet suits; instead, we wrapped towels around our waists and sat our damp bottoms in the car. I found snacks in the bottom of one of the many bags required to take multiple children to the pool. The snacks were warm and melty, but they'd fill tummies for a few minutes. I passed them out to the eager hands behind me and pulled the seat belt across my chest, acutely aware of how my arms and hands worked to perform these simple tasks I usually took for granted. We were not even out of the parking lot when I heard a question from the backseat.

"Mom?"

"Yes."

"You know that boy?"

I took a deep breath. "Which one?"

"The one with the younger brothers."

Well, that didn't take long. I had wondered if there would be questions about one of the boys in our group, a recent amputee who had been wheeled up to the pool, ready for some birthday party fun. A pool is not a place to hide your body, and this young man surprised me with his apparent comfort in this public situation. As I'd looked down at his prosthetic legs leaning up against his wheelchair, I'd wondered if my girls would have questions.

"Yes, what about him?" I braced myself for a serious conversation about body differences and disability and kindness.

"He had a lot of chips! Two bags!"

Of course that's what this chip-loving daughter of mine would notice! While I was concerned about heavy topics and big feelings, she had silently been acting as the self-appointed chip-fairness police and was counting how many snack-sized bags of chips every child at the party got to have.

"Well, he's older than you, so he could have more." And as far as I was concerned, this boy could have as many bags of Cheetos as he wanted.

I tend to go heavy quickly. I don't do small talk well. I've never been accused of being the fun one in the group or of being too shallow. But I have been accused of being overly intense, too serious, even cold and intimidating (that darn furrowed brow!). So part of this journey in learning to love my actual neighbors has, for me, involved lightening up.

We Christians can collectively be too serious about too much of life. We look at the amputated limb and forget about the pool and the chips. But not this boy and his peers. In a situation that had the potential to feel uncomfortable, he likely felt some semblance of normal tween life as he sat munching massive amounts of Cheetos poolside. Other boys were in the pool with him, splashing him in the face . . . and he was laughing. Here's the thing: we can make other people feel welcome and comfortable if we have fun with them.

Once again 2 Peter offers us direction in our pursuit of loving our neighbor: add "mutual affection" or "warm friendliness" to our faith. We are to care for one another with warmth and friendliness. The idea of *lightening up* reminds us of the basics of heartfelt rapport in relationships: laughing, smiling, even common courtesy. This practice can help us serious types understand when to keep connections natural and enjoyable. If we want to allow for friendship, for that "mutual affection" to bubble up, we must have some points of levity with plain fun.

Laughing Together

When Derek and I started dating, he had a picture in his apartment at the Dale House of what is known as *Laughing Jesus*. It's a sketch of Jesus with his head thrown back, his mouth open, having a good laugh. There is joy there. Over twenty years later, the picture still takes me off guard because it's not how I think of Jesus or how I see him reflected in other depictions. He is often on the cross (not a laughable moment), and usually his face is neutral or even stern. The occasional picture of Jesus with children will have the hint of a smile, but a laughing Jesus takes us by surprise. Perhaps that says something about what we as Jesus followers are known for. We reflect him through art, or simply our language or tone of voice, with a serious bent. We are often known for our no, for what we are against. And yet we are for freedom. We are for love. We are for peace. We are for the good things of this life. We may not always recognize it, but we are also for fun.

Laughter and humor can cut the tension in the moment. Sometimes people need a reprieve from the intensity, whether we're in the middle of a one-on-one conversation or a group discussion, or we're giving a talk in front of a group. We've all been there, feeling the weight of the subject matter or the conflict creating a pressure-cooker environment. Then someone cracks a joke, and there is a collective sigh of relief that the awkwardness has been acknowledged and at least we can still laugh together.

Scott Weems, author of *Ha! The Science of When We Laugh and Why*, explains that humor stems from our brains being confused about how to respond, which is why we often laugh at inappropriate times. "Whatever causes our brain confusion or conflict is likely to make us laugh," he says. "And we all laugh at different things because we each have different thresholds for what leads to confusion, and what offends us deeply."[1] Being mindful of this confusion helps me when I think my neighbor's laughter is inappropriate or when I realize I'm the only one laughing. In other words, for me, *lightening up* includes allowing other people to find things funny when I don't and not getting offended.

Apart from single moments, we need humor to create connection points. Self-deprecating humor puts the speaker at the butt end of the joke. That shows a willingness to laugh at one's self, circumstances, or biases, or at the uncomfortable dynamics at play. Self-deprecating humor takes away the most potential to offend. It lets the other person know that our desire to laugh with them is more important than our pride.

As for the *Laughing Jesus*, it now sits in Derek's office. A place where people come in with deep hurts from life: abuse, homelessness, addiction, and trauma. It's easy for him to get bogged down with the pain of the world. And yet as a person standing in that Holy Saturday space, Derek is also tied to the hope of heaven. This picture reminds him of the joy and delight God finds in his people, regardless of their circumstances.

When Church Is a Party

Our church's name, Celebration Community Church, shows we like to have fun. In case that's not clear enough, our tagline is "A Fun Place to Get Serious about God," and our URL really brings it home: thepartychurch.com. As the overthinker (read, overly serious) follower of Jesus, I would never have imagined being part of a church that called itself "the party church." The gospel is no joke, after all. Despite my hesitation, the first service we attended felt like home, making my need to lighten up that much more evident. Celebration, as we call it, is hardly a stodgy place, but it is serious about God. The two don't have to be mutually exclusive. I'm still learning that.

We are "the party church" based on the biblical story of the prodigal son. The son returns to his father's home after making some self-destructive decisions. His father's response?

He throws a party. He does not focus on what has happened in the past but celebrates the reunion and anticipates how they will move forward together. We believe the story represents our heavenly Father and the delight and joy he experiences when we return to him.

The other reason we claim "the party church" title is we like to throw parties for each other and the neighborhood. A trunk-or-treat event in the parking lot, a baby shower, a barbecue or two. All with the idea that people, our neighbors included, are worth celebrating. God rejoices in his creation. We do too. As we celebrate and worship the God who made us, we celebrate the people right in front of us.

Jesus was here on earth for serious business. His mission? To take on the sin of the world and overcome it. Yet the very first miracle he performed was at a wedding—a party! And what was the miracle he chose to perform? He turned water into wine (see John 2).

Jesus had his pick of miracles that evening. He could have pulled out his healing tricks or cast out a few demons as he'd later do, but he didn't want to stop the celebration. The party was about to come to a screeching halt; they'd run out of wine. Jesus could have taken this moment and turned it into a serious matter: a public miracle. And yet he indicated to his mother that he wasn't ready to make a big fuss with his miracle-making skills. Through his discretion, he let the party continue. Only the people who brought him the water jugs knew what he'd done.

I picture Jesus walking away from the reception still in full swing, the music and laughter going up into the night sky, knowing things were about to get real as word spread that he'd performed a miracle. Here's what I take away from this story: *Jesus was at the wedding.* He was in the middle of the party. Maybe he wasn't hitting the dance floor, or maybe he was—we don't know. But we do know he was there with people to celebrate a life marker.

The wine mattered. When Jesus's mother, Mary, came to him in a panic, she knew a major party foul was about to happen. She expressed an urgency that it needed to be fixed. And though Jesus didn't feel he could make a big scene with the miracle, he was willing to out himself because it was important to the people who were there.

We can spend much of our time deciding what is worth our time, even what is worth God's attention. The self-appointed importance enforcers, we manage the hierarchy of weight for the issues we discuss. But Jesus knew the celebration mattered. He could have said he was saving his first miracle for the hard hitters, not some party drinks. But what matters to us, the people he loves, matters to him. We can come to him with an urgency that may be seen as frivolous, but if it's our desire, he wants to hear because that's what relationship is about.

Sometimes *lightening up* means asking God for those things our neighbors want that are important to them, no matter how small they seem to us. Other times it means making the little connection points important too.

Small Connections Matter

I handed my Costco credit card to the checker. It was Monday of Easter week and the store was gearing up for a busy few days. My youngest two ran off to watch the pizza maker through the café window, and I said, "The only problem is I can't do all of my Easter shopping with them here." I pointed in their direction. "I think I'll need to come back for their Easter basket stuff."

"Oh, I know what you mean." Her hands kept moving as she talked. She picked up the giant jar of pickles from my cart and scanned the barcode. *Beep.* "I bought my Easter gifts for my grandkids already. Did you see the dresses?" She motioned toward the back of the store. "They are so cute! And I got one for each of my girls." Granola bars scanned. *Beep.*

"I'll have to look when I come back." The reality that I would need to come back to this same store in the next few days was sinking in. "I wanted to get some of those flowers anyway. They are beautiful." An army's worth of chicken breasts scanned. *Beep.*

"Those go fast." Her tone was one of warning. An insider letting me know I shouldn't depend on finding tomorrow what I saw today. I nodded. I was taking her warning to heart.

Not rocket science. Not earth shattering. Simply sharing the mundane details of the week ahead. I could bond with my new grandma friend over Easter dresses and chocolate eggs. Or not. As she handed me my receipt, she paused and looked at me. "Have a great week, sweetie."

We knew we'd made a connection. I saw her as a person outside of her job. She saw me as more than one more bulk toilet paper purchaser to get through her line. It's the small details that help us notice the people right in front of us. This is showing love. We often think of the grand gestures when loving our neighbors, the things that require sacrifice, but *lightening up* includes seeing the small gestures as equally important in building relationships.

My neighbors across the street have three children. Our lives parallel each other's because of our stage of life. We can laugh at potty-training disasters and childcare mix-ups, and we carpool to the elementary school. Two doors down from them is a single man who shares Derek's love for the University of Colorado football program. Let's just say they can talk strategy and stats. Our neighbor behind us lives in her parents' old home, never had children of her own, and has adopted our girls as her default grandchildren. We share a love of the neighborhood's history, Italian food, and family.

With some people the connection points are easy to find, and with others it takes a little more work. We have to be intentional about searching out places of shared interest and then jump on them when we discover them.

Common ground is where the enjoyable lives. When we first meet someone, we likely start at this place, but we need to come back to it again and again. When we feel the heavy starting to take over, we can revisit the points we have in common and remember to lighten up, because relationships aren't supposed to be forced. They're supposed to feel somewhat natural.

When we connect on lighter matters, we can remember our neighbors aren't just people we are obligated to love; they are people we can enjoy. If we've moved through awkward moments and stuck it out, we've moved toward deeper relationship and toward love.

It is a human longing to belong, and finding common points of interest allows for that. Belonging is not one-way; it is mutual. We are here not just to serve our neighbors but to receive from them as well. We recognize our own need for belonging when we allow our neighbors to love us in return. And we usually find they have much to teach us in what it means to love.

Natural Connection Points with Your Actual Neighbors

Proximity. You live on the same block, in the same townhome development, on the same cul-de-sac. These shared spaces require some communication. Whether it's construction on your street or the day the trash gets picked up, your proximity offers neighborly connection points.

Geography. The rainstorm washed away some gravel. The heat wave is making all of the apartments sweltering. The full moon lit up your backyard. The mountains or beach or park down the street are incredibly beautiful. These are part of God's creation that you and your neighbors have in common.

Allowing Space for Mutual Affection

Our neighbors have not asked to be our love project; they likely want to be known and appreciated. We lighten up when we remember we are not their savior (we always come back to humility, remembering who we are and who God is) but rather that God made us for one another and to enjoy one another. In order for us to have "mutual affection," we must be pursuing two-way relationships.

As part of the "revitalization committee" for the school, I was expected to get the word out in the neighborhood about the changes under way. Pregnant, with a two-year-old

Stage of life. You are both college students, pregnant, starting a business, approaching retirement. From parenting toddlers to caring for elderly parents, if you share one aspect of a stage of life, you likely share many details about your day-to-day experiences.

Common cause. From raising money for local schools to rallying around a neighbor in need of support, if you share a passion for an issue, an event, or a larger purpose, you have natural connection points with your neighbors. From campaigning for a local ballot issue to thanking a coach or teacher, you can all come together under a common mission.

Interests. This is just plain old fun. Restoring cars. Cake decorating. Watching the latest reality TV show. These are the details that can bind you together and be your relationship go-to, which will then lead to other natural offshoots.

strapped into the stroller, I walked block by block, knocking on doors that mostly went unopened.

As I approached a duplex I saw the signs of a family: toys on the front steps, baby pool on the lawn. This was my target audience. I knocked on the door. A woman answered and out bolted a two-year-old ball of spunk (if you know two-year-olds, you know what I mean). The woman saw my bulging stomach, and we knew we could connect.

Her English was limited, but my four years as a Spanish major were not about to go to waste. We quickly switched to Spanish. I told her about the changes at the school. She listened with quiet politeness, but I could tell the details that were debated with fervor at our Wednesday evening meetings seemed moot to her. Soon we were on to other topics—mostly that she was lonely. I knew I could help with that. I had my own network of moms, so I invited her to my church's MOPS (Mothers of Preschoolers) group. I was going to out-friend, out-connect, out-love this woman.

I only lived a few blocks away, so over the next few months we walked and talked, both of us pushing strollers. I knew she was lonely, but the details she shared during our walks around the lake confirmed just how much and offered me perspective on my own woes. She hadn't seen her family in Mexico in years; her own mother had never met her children. Her husband would leave for a night at a time and she didn't know where he went. She felt trapped in a country where she didn't understand the systems or the language. I felt helpless other than to go on those walks and to arrange for someone with extra seats in their minivan to give her a ride to MOPS.

My life felt overly privileged, comfortable, in comparison to hers. Complaining or talking about my marriage stressors seemed inappropriate. Until one day she said something that made me realize I wasn't giving her a full picture of my life. I'd been worried about sounding ungrateful, bratty even, by sharing what kept me up at night. But my silence implied I had no problems at all. Realizing this, I told her some of my pregnancy-related worries, places where my husband was struggling, where I was struggling. Our relationship shifted in that moment. I was showing her I had needs. In other words, in *lightening up*, I let her be my friend.

As we love the people right in front of us, we need to allow space for the mutual part. That Protestant work ethic can get the best of us, and we can program our love with our agendas until there is nothing organic or natural left. A one-sided relationship is not a relationship; it is a project, and people are not our projects. When we allow God to be God, we have freedom to love our neighbors without assuming a parental or authoritative role. Mutual affection doesn't always happen. Our neighbors aren't necessarily interested in a relationship with us. However, if we approach everyone as a potential friend, even a potential mentor, we will be the richer for it, and I believe our neighbors will experience our love in an honoring way.

At Dry Bones Denver, the staff refer to the kids they work with on the street as "friends." Not "clients" or "homeless kids" or "runaways," but "friends." This simple word choice sets an organizational tone. Whether someone is on paid staff, a volunteer, or a "friend on the streets," the message is being sent that there is a give-and-take along the entire relationship.

Our word choice makes a difference in showing mutual affection—as does sharing everyday experiences such as eating. Food is both a basic need and a social opportunity. It is nonthreatening, a lighter encounter that levels the playing field and establishes a peer dynamic, or "mutual affection."

The Food Factor

There is something about handing someone something to eat that lightens the moment. Food expresses love in a tangible way because it meets physical needs, but it also helps people let their guard down as they eat together. Whether you're bringing orange slices to the soccer sidelines or hosting a Saturday brunch in your backyard, food can say, "I thought of you. I knew you would be here. I prepared for you."

We have snacks at our Sunday church services every week. That sounds like a few pretzels in a bowl and maybe some juice boxes. But it feels more like a buffet, the way the line winds past the kitchen and people carry their little plates of baby carrots and mini muffins to their chairs. Celebration's come-as-you-are casual vibe means come with appetites too. Our worship space is not sterile; it is filled with crumbs, and water cups that spill, and kids who want a midmorning snack even though their parents fed them a proper breakfast earlier. It's also an easy way for members of the congregation to serve each other. This is a rotating job that our family performs only a couple of times a year, but we benefit from it every Sunday we are present.

Eating a meal together can ultimately foster relationships. My friend Sarah doesn't have a big house, but her backyard can welcome people much of the year with the Dallas weather. She wanted to meet her neighbors and needed a table large enough to seat a number of guests, so she asked her dad to build one. She hosted a dinner. Neighbors came. She hosted more dinners and more people came, often asking if they could invite a friend.

Knowing Sarah, I know why they asked. She would be the first to say it's not about the food, it's about the people. Sarah has a knack for seeing someone, remembering details they tell her in a brief conversation, and making connections with them as she introduces them to others. The meal is not a fuss. However, the people are. The meal offers an opportunity to bring new friends together. She started a movement called Neighbor's Table (see www.neighborstable.com), and she is now delivering tables around the country because people are seeing that sometimes the best way to love someone is around a table.

Food is universal, but not all food is the same. In high school I spent a summer in Costa Rica and ate black beans and rice at least two meals a day. *Gallo pinto*, as the mixture is called, was a culinary staple my host mother offered with love. She soaked the beans and cooked the rice so I might have a bit of my host country's flavor. When we sit in someone's kitchen or backyard or next to them in the office break room, we can appreciate new food. Their offering may be more than just a snack. It can be a lesson in culture, finances, traditions, and preferences. We can accept the gift of food flippantly or with care and appreciation, recognizing food can represent many facets of a person.

In the spirit of friendship and mutual relationship, we must not only extend invitations for shared meals; we must also accept our neighbors' invitations, allowing them to host us. Jesus certainly did. He went to all kinds of homes, ate with a few thousand people on the beach, and used food and wine as a symbol for us to remember him by throughout history.

Matt and Nikki, the founders of Dry Bones Denver, understand the generous gesture that sharing food can be. One day as they were out looking for their friends on Denver's streets, they found a few. Many kids eat the leftovers of people walking by. Restaurant goers who leave with take-out boxes in hand sometimes offer the food to kids who are panhandling. Matt and Nikki recognized the Styrofoam box in one friend's hand and noticed he was thoroughly enjoying his burger.

"That looks good," Matt commented.

The young man extended his half-eaten burger toward Matt and Nikki. "Here," he offered. "Have some."

Their stomachs turned a bit at the thought of biting into the already twice-germed sandwich, but they also recognized

Ways to Use Food to Connect

Celebrate a milestone. A baby coming, a graduation, a good report card—celebrate what you know is important to your neighbor. Whether you host the celebration in your home or church or you bring the party to them, most people love the sentiment of celebration (even if they don't love being the center of attention).

Meet a basic need. A food bank, garden collective, or soup kitchen can meet the most basic need for food in your community. Use your resources to let your neighbors know they are not forgotten. Whether you are part of a group that hosts the food bank or a family who works at the soup kitchen, you are showing your neighbors their needs matter to you.

Meet an immediate need. Though someone may be able to afford food, they may also be in the middle of a crisis where shopping and cooking are just more things that must be attended to. A hospitalization, a new baby, or a death in the

this moment for what it was: their friend had been unexpectedly blessed in abundance and wanted to share his blessing with them. He didn't know where his next meal would come from, yet he was willing to share what little he had with them. This young man's generosity made the widow's mite look stingy. Matt and Nikki couldn't turn down such a heartfelt offer, so they sat down and each took a bite from the burger, grateful most of it had already been consumed.

family distract people from their daily tasks. Helping with meals during that time can be a great gift.

Anticipate a need. When you know a big event is coming up (surgery or wedding) or it's an especially busy time of year (tax season for your accountant neighbor), make some meals that can go in the freezer and be pulled out in a pinch, or arrange a schedule with a group to bring meals over a period of time.

Offer a thank-you. A neighbor took care of your family lizard and you want to say "thanks"; take them some cinnamon rolls. Someone could use some recognition; throw them a party. Celebrations almost always include food. And nothing says "thank you" like a home-cooked meal.

Have great conversations. Over and over we see stories in the Bible about people connecting through shared meals. The same is true today of cultures around the world. Have a neighbor or neighbors over for dinner, sit down together, and ask questions and learn. It is a timeless, and increasingly rare, way to connect.

Fun Can Be the End Goal

Laughter is fun. Parties are fun. Food can be fun. Offering more fun to our neighbors is a good thing. If we are aiming to close divides and build bridges, fun may be just the key. In fact, why don't we go ahead and make it the goal sometimes? Whether neighbor to neighbor or as a group, throw a party, be silly, laugh together. Make fun the goal.

All year the congregation of Southeast Christian Church in Parker, Colorado, is encouraged to build relationships with the people right in front of them. In fact, part of their mission statement says, "We love like Jesus where we live." But one day a year is set aside for the "Love Where You Live" campaign. Families serve together with a lighthearted approach. The guidelines: love your neighbors, with no pressure to talk to them about Jesus or invite them to church. The church's leadership realized many congregants associated service with evangelism. But when the church gave permission not to talk about faith or church, people's hesitation to participate went away, and they were able to focus on the fun of loving without expectations.

In this single day of service, families are grouped together and given packets with a few supplies (for example, Sharpies, sticky notes, balloons, and $100 cash) and ideas on ways to show neighbors love in different parts of town. Groups are sent out to various locations from parks to grocery stores with the challenge to get creative when making their neighbors smile. From taking dog treats to the local dog park to leaving encouraging notes on windshields in a parking lot to paying for someone's groceries, these groups put the emphasis on spreading a little happiness.

The church's long-term goal with this activity is to get the congregation thinking about how they can show love in small ways to the people right in front of them. It's a day to spark thinking, conversation, and even a little of the awkward, so people know they can lighten up with their neighbors without an elaborate plan. They *can* give neighbors flowers on a random day. They *can* compliment someone on their smile. They *can* use the halftime break at a soccer game to quickly pick up trash at the park. It's as simple as taking the initiative to do something kind.

Some of the church's families have taken on this effort on a more regular basis. Small groups have adopted the local fire station and take the firefighters dinner on rotation. Families have made cookies for their neighbors. Because it's a practice, the more they do it, the more natural it feels.

While practice does help, *lightening up* and having fun are not always easy. From personalities to past conflict, there are many reasons why they may feel more difficult in certain situations or relationships. But we still need to work toward that goal, even if the laughter and fun don't come automatically.

When Lightening Up Is Difficult

"Just lighten up!" Brittany remembers that phrase being thrown out to her as a teenager, never offered as a compliment. She now bristles at those words, feeling the familiar defensiveness creep in.

Even if this concept of *lightening up* doesn't trigger something deeper, the very idea can feel difficult, nearly impossible, if we are hitting on deeply held beliefs or are in conversation with someone who is pushing our buttons. We might feel our body tighten, jaw clench, and heart rate increase as the conversation escalates. The furrowed brow digs in, the arms cross, and we begin to feel flustered.

If we can't control what the other person is saying, doing, or believing, and they aren't interested in "mutual affection," why try? Tense moments pop up, and they are decision points for our response. If we want to stay in relationship with this person, we need to evaluate if escalating or de-escalating will serve us best in the long term. Sometimes that tense moment is the right time to address an issue head-on, and sometimes tabling the topic for a more appropriate time, place, and audience is the best idea.

We each have our own opinions, ideas, and perspectives. Naturally we believe the ones we hold are the most valid, or we wouldn't hold them, right? Moving toward "warm friendliness" may not come naturally if we go on our feelings alone. But if we lead with a disciplined approach toward respect, feelings may follow. This is not a call to stay in a hurtful situation but to work toward friendliness and building bridges when possible. Remember that the larger goal of *lightening up* is positive connection.

When It's More Like Tensing Up

If you'd like to lighten up but can't get past your anger or frustration with the person in front of you, try a few of these approaches.

Breathe. Focusing on your breaths and slowing them down can help your body out of its fight-or-flight mode. You may feel like doing both fight and flight, but your resolve is telling you to stay. Breathing will help make that possible.

Change course. Or subject. Or location. You are not required to debate the latest controversy or political issue. You have freedom to change the subject or to get out of the conversation. If you don't feel that freedom, it's a conversation you should probably leave anyway.

A CALL TO
Saturday Living

May we be people known for our joy as much as we are known for our work. The church has a reputation for being about serious business, but maybe it's time for us to have a reputation for fun too, for *lightening up*. Everyone needs to eat, to laugh, and to be celebrated. As God's people we can help with all of those things. In a time where we don't have to go looking for bad news, may we find some good things to commemorate and applaud as a form of love. We have good news to celebrate; may we be known for doing that well.

Get perspective. In the moment, this discussion—and the topics and viewpoints it represents—may feel like the most important thing in the world. Maybe it is. But make sure you're willing to die on that hill before you do. Ask yourself, *Will this matter a year from now? Ten years from now?*

Believe the best. If you start from a place of believing the other person's motives are good, you can look past a lot of minor offenses. If you can't in good faith make that assumption about the person in front of you, you can always remember this is a person made in God's image who uniquely reflects the Creator.

Remember what you appreciate. He's spontaneous. She's generous. He takes care of his flowers. She feeds your cat when you're gone. It might take a little stretching (and humor), but you can come up with at least five things you appreciate about your neighbor. I promise.

Saturday living is about holding the good and the difficult at the same time. May we hold the tension of the real problems of the world with the beauty all around us. May we let down our guard and let our neighbors love us right back. May we let go of our self-importance and loosen up about places where we may disagree. May we take ourselves less seriously since we are here with our neighbors only because of God's gracious allowance.

May we tell that joke, throw that party, have some fun with our neighbors. Because they need to see we are real people who snort when we laugh and make mistakes when we're parenting and get disappointed with life. Because real people in real circumstances who worship a real God is what will show them the hope of Sunday.

This is Saturday living.

—— Questions for *Reflection* ——

1. Would you describe yourself as being on the more serious or the more lighthearted end of the spectrum? How would other people describe you?

2. What is one activity or area of your life that makes your heart lighter? How can you connect with neighbors on this front?

3. Do you see your neighbors as projects or assignments? Or as potential friends? How can you approach strangers as potential friends?

4. How can you connect with your neighbors through food?

5. How can you allow your neighbors to love you?

—— Practicing the *Practice* ——

- Meditate on how Jesus delights in the good things of this life.
- Create meals that can be shared with those around you. From potlucks to cookies and milk, double whatever you're already making.
- Take note of things you have in common with your neighbors so you can connect with them in those areas.
- Give yourself permission to make a mistake or look foolish when loving your neighbor. Laugh when things don't go as planned.
- Allow your neighbors to love you in practical ways. Accept their invitations to host you or care for you.
- Find ways to keep the tone of your interaction light when you're with neighbors who try your patience. Think through your approach ahead of time when emotions are cool.

—— Scripture to *Digest* ——

So I recommend having fun, because there is nothing better for people in this world than to eat, drink, and enjoy life. That way they will experience some happiness along with all the hard work God gives them under the sun. (Eccles. 8:15 NLT)

7

Giving Freely

We make a living by what we get, but we make a life by what we give.

Winston Churchill

A generous person will prosper;
  whoever refreshes others will be refreshed.

Proverbs 11:25

Every store I walked into, I was approached with the same innocent question: "Are you looking for anything in particular?"

Half the time I was able to muster an answer before the tears started again. "Something black. Not sleeveless." Sometimes I'd say, "For a funeral" to give the general picture.

Naturally the salespeople all assumed I was shopping for myself. In every store the response was like their initial question—the same. "Oh, I'm sorry. What size are you?"

That's when the tears would come if they hadn't already. "Oh no. It's not for me. For my friend. Her husband died. I need to find a dress tonight. The burial is tomorrow."

The weight of this job felt unbearable. *How did I get here?* I kept thinking. I don't know how to buy a dress for a widow. How do you choose what someone is meant to wear to her husband's funeral?

Earlier that afternoon I'd stopped at Heather's house. Her sister had flown in from the other side of the world. Family friends from states away were arriving, bittersweet reunions taking over her little house. All I wanted was to be helpful in some way.

Heather and I weren't the closest of friends. We'd met when our oldest girls started soccer together at the rec center. We had a genuine connection, but the busyness of multiple kids and life as soccer moms kept us from seeing each other beyond the school playground during the rush of pickups. We'd reconnected in the last few weeks. Her husband, Jon, had been hospitalized unexpectedly, and I'd been helping her with childcare while she was at the hospital. When I learned he had died, my grief for her—now a widow with three young children—made me want to rip my heart out. It felt unbearable. And so I wanted to do something.

"What are you going to do tonight?" I'd asked her.

"Well, we might go to the mall." She looked like she hadn't slept in a week. She probably hadn't.

"Does that sound good to you?" I couldn't imagine it would, but maybe distraction was what she was looking for.

"No," she answered. "My mom needs a few things."

"I can take her. Or get whatever she needs. Just tell me." She looked away.

"What are you going to wear tomorrow?" I asked.

"I don't know. I looked in my closet, but I don't know. I should wear a black dress, right?" She paused. "I don't have anything like that."

"I'll go to the mall," I said. "I'll find you something. You stay with your mom."

How could she possibly spend tonight at the mall? It was the most no-brainer offer I could ever make. She didn't want to put me out. *Are you kidding me?* I wanted to scream. I resisted the yelling and reassured her I wanted to do this. Truly. I got her sizes and preferences. She needed two dresses: one for the burial and another for the memorial service.

Other moms in the neighborhood had already started an email thread about ways to support Heather. I proposed the group pool money to buy these outfits for her; they agreed. And so I walked from store to store, crying my way through the mall, buying dresses, jewelry, shoes, knowing I could return what she didn't like. A phone call from another mom, giving me tips, reminding me not to buy something too frumpy or too cheap (I think she was a little concerned I was the one on this most important dress-finding mission), was "the village" cheering me on. Heather deserved to put on something special for these occasions.

Considering her reality, my task seemed both frivolous and important. A dress? Who cares when her whole life just got upended? And yet because I was at arm's length, not part of her inner circle, she didn't need me sitting with her. People had traveled from across the country and the world to do that. She needed practical help. She needed two dresses. Though I had babies at home who needed to be cared for, though I hated the mall, though I wanted to go home and numb my own sadness for my friend with food or wine or YouTube, I knew this was something I not only should do but wanted to. My time, money, and energy were all hers. And because of the generous giving of the neighborhood mamas, I had the power to make the shopping spree happen.

Standing on Heather's porch, I knew I would do anything in my power to help her. I couldn't offer what she really wanted, to bring her husband back, but I'd asked questions and heard a need. I was willing to have repeated uncomfortable conversations with well-meaning salespeople. I could deal with the reality of my neighbor's situation, accepting what I could not change, to offer a few beautiful things on some very dark days. My walk through the mall was the culmination of all the previous practices. It was my love march on Heather's behalf.

The final instruction we receive in 2 Peter 1:5–9 is to add "love" or "generous love" to all the other practices. Love is the cherry on top after we do the hard work of getting to this point. When we've humbled ourselves, asked questions, truly listened, stayed in uncomfortable situations, dealt with our neighbor's reality, and allowed a friendship to grow, love and generosity are appropriate (and usually welcomed). When we give freely, we aren't holding back. We aren't worried about whether there will be enough to go around. We are living from the perspective that every good gift is from God (James 1:17), and so we can hold it lightly and offer it back to God to be used for his purposes.

That night as I delivered my shopping spoils and Heather and I shared more tears as she held up each dress, we moved one step further into friendship. *Giving freely*, when done in the context of the other practices, has a way of binding hearts, because it is done out of seeing and knowing the person right in front of us.

But what prompts us to give freely? Often we feel compelled out of compassion or genuine care for our neighbor. The underlying spirit of *giving freely*, generously, is gratitude. As Christians we give because we've been given to. We know grace is a gift, and out of appreciation or gratitude we are compelled to give to those around us. Not because they've earned it but because we know every good thing we have belongs to God anyway. Gratitude may not come instinctively, but it can be cultivated, which will in turn allow us to give freely.

Gratitude Fuels Generosity

From Harvard Health to *Psychology Today*, it's not hard to find research that concludes gratitude is good for us.[1] Science confirms what Scripture tells us: giving thanks helps us thrive as people. "Give thanks in all circumstances; for this is God's will for you in Christ Jesus" (1 Thess. 5:18). When we give thanks freely to God for the gifts he has provided, we walk through our days with a lighter spirit. We are more aware of what we have. We are grateful people because we know we have been reconciled to God through Christ. He has given us life twice over, and this is good news, regardless of what our day or stress level holds. Out of gratitude for these enormous gifts, we desire to return that generous love to our neighbors. We want to thank God by loving the people he loves. That was true for my friend Kendra.

Kendra met some local Afghan refugee families in her community. Thanksgiving was approaching, and she wanted to share the holiday spirit with her new neighbors and introduce them to her family. So she invited them (two families and a few cousins) over for a pre-holiday brunch. In preparation for their meal together, Kendra spread a tablecloth on the living room floor so they could eat together Afghan style. Twelve guests and Kendra's family of five took their spots on the floor.

Before they ate, Kendra brought out champagne flutes filled with sparkling cider and asked her guests if they knew what a toast was. They didn't. So she demonstrated by raising her filled glass and saying how grateful she was for them. They all said "Cheers" as they clinked glasses. Kendra's husband, Eric, then offered a similar toast: "I want you to know that I'm glad you're here with us in our country, and you are always welcome in our home."

Later as the kids kicked the soccer ball and jumped on the trampoline in the backyard, Kendra's heart continued to beat in gratitude for life, unexpected intersections, and new friendships.

Though she didn't know exactly what to do or how to do it, Kendra wanted to extend a warm welcome to this family new to her community. She wasn't pretending away the hard realities of their lives. She knew living in a new country with few resources isn't easy. She recognized their potential isolation and so made a place of belonging for them. The gratitude that overflowed Kendra's heart prompted her to point her neighbors toward hope with an invitation of love.

As I consider what I want to be known for, generosity is at the top of the list. Why? Because I have been given to generously. Gratitude fuels my desire to love and, I pray, overflows to how I treat those around me—and to how much I give of what I have.

Giving What We Have

When we consider generosity, we often think of financial giving. But our attention, time, influence, skills, and resources can all be given for our neighbors' benefit. As Derek talks with people about the work of Providence Network, he offers them the opportunity to give their time, talent, and treasure to the greater good. People volunteer to watch children as their moms are in counseling. They make dinner and eat with the residents of a home once a month so they can maintain long-term relationships with new friends. They give from their savings and estates and extra spending money so lights can be kept on and furnaces repaired.

No matter the number of zeros on the check, if we are giving from a heart of sharing and generosity, God sees that. We find this in Scripture. As people encountered Jesus and received healing or freedom, they understood the magnitude of the gift they'd received. It was out of gratitude for what he offered that they generously gave back to him.

One woman's understanding that Jesus changed everything prompted her to give everything. She walked into a party carrying her jar of perfume. It was worth a lot, maybe enough to cover her expenses for a year. There was Jesus eating dinner—he was her target. She broke open the jar and placed the oil on his head, anointing him. Others at the party got upset, gasped even, not because she was touching Jesus but because of what the oil was worth. How dare she give so freely when the money could be used to help the poor? I admit that sounds like a pretty good argument, one I've made before when seeing what I considered frivolous spending.

But Jesus stopped them. "Let her alone. Why are you giving her a hard time? She has just done something wonderfully significant for me" (Mark 14:6 MSG). This woman considered what she had to give and gave it with abandon. She gave Jesus all she could. This was days before his death, so this woman did not know all that he was about to do for her. What compelled her to give such an over-the-top gift? I'm not sure, but Jesus welcomed the generous, free gesture of love. He continued, "You can be sure that wherever in the whole world the Message is preached, what she just did is going to be talked about admiringly" (v. 9 MSG). And yes, here we are today still remembering her.

I have a front-row seat to the church being generous, friends and acquaintances who respond when they feel God prompting them to share. A year after moving into their house, my friends Jeff and Heidi got some new next-door neighbors: a woman with a few kids. A single mom? It was unclear, but soon there were more kids living with their neighbor, and then even more. After a year of neighborly small talk, Jeff and Heidi realized they were living next to a group home for boys. The boys were not necessarily related by blood, but now because of their circumstances, they shared a home. And as boys tend to do, they were outside a lot, trying to expel some energy.

Jeff and Heidi had a small basketball court in their backyard, so they invited the boys to come over and play. As the boys grew and more teenagers started moving in, Jeff and Heidi could see the little court was no longer big enough. They needed a big one where multiple man-sized children could run up and down, getting out that collective energy while preserving some childhood fun. Jeff and Heidi considered their own backyard and their neighbor's much smaller yard and decided theirs was more suitable for the large court. Though the larger footprint would nearly cover their small backyard with concrete, they knew there was a need they could fill. So they measured out the specs, poured the concrete, and installed hoops on either end. They created some house rules about when the boys could be over (after dark the court was closed), and they shared their backyard with their neighbors.

Did they give up their landscaping options? Yes. Some of their privacy? Yes. This very tangible way of showing love to the boys next door (and to their hardworking house mother, who needed them to blow off some steam) was not without sacrifice. But Jeff and Heidi also had the sense God had given them more than plenty, he had provided, and the proper response out of gratitude was to share generously.

When I think of generous giving I often go to the physical, those things my neighbor can see, taste, and touch. But there are many ways to offer love and give freely that cannot be measured in bank accounts or posted on Instagram, yet they are more valuable. Just as we give generously of our time, talent, and treasure, we give mercy and grace out of gratitude for what we have already received.

Offering Mercy and Grace

There has been a bump in car break-ins in my neighborhood in the last year—increased "crimes of opportunity" as thieves are finding more valuable contents left in plain view. Perhaps this is the by-product of the continued rise in the average household income combined with new residents not accustomed to city living. As a result the neighborhood message board has hosted multiple threads about how to deal with this reality.

One victim shared her conversation with the Denver police officer who came to investigate her break-in. "Get to know your neighbors," he said. "When you know who they are and they know you, they are more likely to pay attention to suspicious activity." The know-your-neighbor sentiment is disappearing. We need to remind one another to know the people right around us, because the common good rises when we watch out for each other.

This prompted another woman to share about her husband catching a boy going through their car parked in their driveway. It was the middle of the day, and the boy's brother stood on the corner acting as watch. Rather than offer the most punitive consequences available, the man sat the two boys on his front steps (how he convinced them to do that is still a mystery to me) and wouldn't let them leave until they disclosed their parents' phone number. He called the parents and waited for them to come get the boys. He was the one they were offending, yet he chose to offer mercy and grace. Rather than calling the police, he told the boys, "Don't do this again," sending them off with a charge to do better. This isn't the right call for every situation, but offering mercy and grace to our neighbors in nonviolent offenses is sometimes appropriate.

Mercy is holding back the punishment someone deserves. Grace is offering kindness that someone doesn't deserve. This pattern is repeated in my life multiple times a day. I stumble. I sin, deciding to make my own way without God. I fall. Though I may experience earthly consequences, he does not punish me. He offers mercy. Not only that, he continues to give me new life every day. He offers grace.

Having experienced this kind of love, I want to extend the same to my neighbors. They let the trash cans overflow in the alley? We may need to have a conversation about it, but I don't need to lash out or harbor anger. If I do, I need to repent. Practical problems can and should be met with practical solutions, but I want to come at them with a belief that God has made us for each other. I am to extend forgiveness to those around me, knowing the measure I'm offering my neighbor is a fraction of the forgiveness God has granted me. This is what it is to give freely.

Offering Forgiveness

I have a friend; I'll call her Lisa. Lisa was in remodel mode. She had the plans for her new fence approved by the city, and the framing was almost complete when the city inspector showed up to inform her they were out of compliance. That same day Lisa's neighbor Holly knocked on her door and for fifteen minutes spewed anger about the fence and its location. Lisa was taken aback. She had no idea her neighbor was mad about the fence. She felt cornered, attacked, and hurt.

It was clear to Lisa and her husband that they needed to scrap the work that had been done and move the location of the fence. As they made new plans and tore down the work already done, the hurt lingered. Lisa had a choice to make: to let the repercussions of the conflict drive a wedge in her friendship with Holly, or to extend grace to her neighbor.

Lisa realized they would likely live next to each other for years to come. They already had a history of friendship years long. She decided she needed to forgive her neighbor for that attacking conversation in the kitchen. She didn't tell Holly she'd forgiven her—she figured Holly wasn't really looking for forgiveness. Rather, she prayed through the process and moved forward.

Forgiveness is a basic tenet to our faith in action. As people who have been forgiven—not from our own efforts or deservedness but through Christ—we know what it is to receive grace, or, as we call it, "unmerited favor." From this forgiven place we have the freedom, even the call, to extend grace to others. And when we do we are freed from the burden of carrying the anger, resentment, and bitterness of past hurts. Forgiveness is neither sudden nor letting someone off the hook for what they are responsible for. It takes time, sometimes years. We are forgiving people because we are forgiven people.

Once in a while we need to extend forgiveness to our neighbor for something out of their control. I may feel tension toward my neighbor because he's white or male or has a special liking for chili dogs. Not because he has personally used those characteristics against me but because other people have, and I am projecting my feelings onto my now unsuspecting neighbor. Am I holding something against my neighbor that is out of their control? Do I need to extend them grace as a result? Is this tension identifying someone else I need to truly forgive? We have both the responsibility not to hold others' transgressions against our actual neighbors and an opportunity to forgive others as a result of our neighbors' presence.

The practice of *giving freely* also involves being willing to seek forgiveness when we have wronged (or are part of a people group that has wronged) our neighbor. In my own family we use the philosophy "quickly and frequently" as our measuring stick for asking each other for forgiveness. If we feel the need to apologize, we try to do it with expediency so the tension doesn't fester. The dog was barking all night? Your cousin blocked your neighbor's driveway with his car? Apologize to your neighbors. In talking with someone, did you learn that Christians or your ethnic group or people from your neighborhood—or any other group you identify with—have wronged that person? Apologize. Your neighbor knows you weren't the offender. They also may need a genuine apology from someone who cares about them. God has placed you right there in front of them. This is what it means to give freely.

For Jesus people, our offers of mercy, grace, and forgiveness are motivated by our knowledge and experience of what he did on the cross: our hope. But we may not know if, when, or how to share this hope with our neighbors.

Sharing Our Hope

As we love our neighbors, it is normal for us to want them to know the source of our love. Since the time Jesus walked this earth, Christians have wondered, debated, and theorized about when, where, and how to share the gospel with those around them. I come back to that verse in 2 Timothy: "But *you*—keep your eye on what you're doing; accept the hard times along with the good; keep the Message alive; do a thorough job as God's servant" (4:5 MSG). To "keep the Message alive," we hold it out for others to see. We don't hide the hope that propels us forward. For us to "keep the Message alive," our actions and words need to be congruent. My neighbors will believe the words I say after they've experienced the love I've committed to.

"I don't know why this is happening, but I believe God is with you in it." I've said some version of this sentiment at the pool, in my dining room, on the sidewalk in front of a friend's house, in texts. I am in relationships with my neighbors for the long haul. I want my life to be a witness to my belief that God loves them and the rest of our neighbors. Every once in a while, it feels natural for me to bring up spiritual matters with people I don't already hear talking about them.

I have knowledge of the gospel today because someone years ago told me about God's love for me. There is a time to say out loud where our hope stems from. If we don't, we aren't offering our neighbors the full picture of who we are or the hope to which we're tethered. We don't need to be embarrassed, just appropriate, when we share our faith. It is a bit of a dance, but one we can offer with credibility and integrity if we've traveled with our neighbors through these practices. If we truly believe the good news, we will want to share it. The question is, when and how?

I'll admit I've inserted spiritual talk into conversations because I've felt I "should," that it was my obligation to bring Jesus into the moment. I have had to unlearn some "shoulds" I've absorbed over the years. I know better now than I did ten or twenty years ago that Jesus *is* part of every moment and conversation, whether I mention him by name or not. The truth is I rarely have spiritual conversations with my neighbors, especially the ones I know only on a casual basis. Why? Because it would feel forced. At the same time I don't hide that I'm a Christian. Maybe it's age or maturity or confidence in who I am, but I also have an increased freedom to speak of what is truly important to me. More often now I ask spiritual questions from the overflow of my heart. I feel more latitude than ever to speak about what's most dear and true and hope-filled to me.

My hope is that when spiritual matters come up, the life I've lived in front of my neighbors will be consistent with my words. That it will be easy for them to believe God's love has transformed me because they see both my very human need (in other words, they know I'm a hot mess) and the desire I have to love them well (by what they have experienced of me to that point).

The practice of *giving freely* is about giving from the hidden places of our hearts and includes our understanding of hope. The spiritual work we do will make us more in tune with the Holy Spirit's leadings, which will help us know when and how to share this hope. The same is true for our acts of service. What we do for our neighbors outside of the public eye makes a difference. It takes the focus off of us, reducing the chance that we are unknowingly motivated by recognition.

The Power in Unseen Work

We are coming full circle in this chapter, back to the first practice, *holding a posture of humility*. What we do for our neighbors is between us and God. Sometimes we do things in public to honor our neighbors in a significant way, to let them know they are seen by a larger community, or to inspire others to do the same. But our motive should never be our own recognition. Jesus even said,

> Be especially careful when you are trying to be good so that you don't make a performance out of it. It might

Speaking of Jesus

When we are called to talk of Jesus, we get nervous about stumbling over our words or offending our neighbor. It's going to be okay. Take a deep breath and remember that talk of faith tends to go better when . . .

> *It is honest.* We don't have all of the answers. We can say what we know with certainty, but we don't know everything. We can share our own questions and doubts. God doesn't expect more than honesty from us.
>
> *It happens over time.* As we deepen our relationships with our neighbors, conversations and topics will be revisited. There is not always an urgency to share the gospel today with words. Remember that every en-

be good theater, but the God who made you won't be applauding.

When you do something for someone else, don't call attention to yourself. You've seen them in action, I'm sure—"playactors" I call them—treating prayer meeting and street corner alike as a stage, acting compassionate as long as someone is watching, playing to the crowds. They get applause, true, but that's all they get. When you help someone out, don't think about how it looks. Just do it— quietly and unobtrusively. That is the way your God, who conceived you in love, working behind the scenes, helps you out. (Matt. 6:1–4 MSG) counter is an opportunity to demonstrate the gospel with actions.

It is natural. "Nice to meet you. Here are the four spiritual laws" is not a natural progression of a conversation. The more we are in mutual relationship with our neighbors, the more natural our discussion will be about how Jesus impacts our life. Forcing spiritual conversations goes against the Holy Spirit's work.

It is Spirit led. On the flip side, when the Holy Spirit is prompting us to bring something up, let's do so with humility. God loves his people. He wants to draw them home. It is not our responsibility to do this work but to be willing partners in our neighbor's journey. We will likely only be a small part in God's long and large plan for the person in front of us.

In an age of likes and followers and retweets and extreme language, we are most likely to hear the loudest voices (often synonymous with the most obnoxious ones). Meanwhile, the humble saints have their heads down, faithfully attending to their work. This is one of my largest frustrations with our current culture. The humble don't get the recognition they deserve because they are, well . . . humble. This has always been true, I'm sure. Humility is defined by not seeking the spotlight, and we now have the technology for the most brash to post and share highlight after highlight of their lives.

There is something about giving anonymously that is good for our souls. We are not created for notoriety, yet we live in a celebrity culture. In terms of our public selves, my friend Francie says, "As low as possible, as long as possible." When God elevates us for recognition, to share a message, an idea, or the needs of those we are serving, we must be prepared for that mantle of responsibility. In the meantime, loving our neighbors off center stage will protect us from the pride that can tear away our integrity.

It's the humble saints who inspire me. I know of families who have given sacrificial financial gifts to Providence Network without seeking any recognition. I see professionals who donate their services and willing hands who work in the church nursery. I see men who mentor and women who fundraise all because they know God loves them and the people right in front of them. They walk through life with their hands open, holding loosely to all they have, knowing any good gift came from God in the first place and was meant to be used for his glory. That's exactly what happens: God is glorified when we love our neighbors freely. People sense they are part of something bigger than just them or us.

But as we give freely, we do not do so without giving something up. In other words, love is not free. It is not all feel-good, easy, and natural. It is often disciplined, difficult, even painful. Loving our neighbor involves sacrificing the things most precious to us: our time, our energy, our attention, our money, our priorities, and our hearts.

Giving Freely Is Costly

Love God and others. It's a simple concept but not always simple to carry out. *Giving freely* can feel loaded. How do we simply give? What is appropriate? How much of ourselves do we offer? Who are we responsible to? And does giving to our neighbors generously somehow impede our ability to give where we are already committed (our families, workplaces, churches, etc.)? For each of us, this is a spiritual journey of asking God to direct us to the things only we can do, and then to give freely.

If we consider humanity's relationship with God, we see his love for us has been costly. From original sin to the fact that we've continued to live severed from him, God has loved us, and we have turned away. And, of course, let us not forget the cross; it was costly. Jesus is the ultimate example of *giving freely*. God is not asking us to do anything he hasn't proven himself committed to. We can give freely knowing he is the source of all we have to give. If every good thing we have is from him, we are merely stewards waiting for an opportunity to do his work this side of heaven.

Though we may know these truths in our heads, we are still people working out the realities in our hearts and actions. That is what this life of faith is. We walk in the tension of real pain and real freedom. At least sometimes our inclination will be to give up. To walk away. But if God has called us to love a neighbor in a particular way, he will give us what we need to carry it out. With that understanding we can give freely.

A CALL TO Saturday Living

May the words of the familiar hymn ring true: "They'll know we are Christians by our love." In a world filled with grief, conflict, stress, and disappointment, may we be people who follow Jesus with a generous love for our neighbors. Let us remember the mercy, grace, forgiveness, and love that Christ has extended to us as we interact with the people right in front of us. May we recognize all that has been given to us and with gratitude and generosity offer it to God to be used for his purposes.

May we do the hard work of the other practices—asking questions and listening, being uncomfortable and accepting our neighbors as they are, and developing honest, mutual relationships with them—so that our *giving freely* is rooted in an understanding of who our neighbors are and how we can best love them. May we be people who offer this love humbly and generously so that our neighbors may experience a taste of Christ's hope through us.

May we not shy away from sharing our hope but offer it to our fellow stumblers, our neighbors doing their best to make life work. We are living in a Good Friday world, but the glory of Resurrection Sunday is within reach. When we freely give to our neighbors, we are conveying that God's grace is for them too.

This is Saturday living.

Questions for *Reflection*

1. What is easy for you to freely give? What is difficult?

2. How are gratitude and generosity connected? What are you grateful for today? How does this translate to loving your neighbor?

3. Is there a neighbor you need to forgive? Is there a neighbor whose forgiveness you need to pursue? If so, what is a next step you can take?

4. How do you feel about spiritual talk with your neighbors? Can you see it as a way of freely giving in love?

5. Where is God asking you to be more generous? How will it cost you?

—— Practicing the *Practice* ——

- List the ways you are grateful for your neighbors.
- Give to someone in the most low-profile way possible. Humility matters as you give.
- Take an inventory of the ways you can freely give your time, talent, and treasure. Make a plan for your next steps.
- Engage in spiritual talk if natural and appropriate.
- Ask God to help you forgive those around you, whether they ask it of you or not.
- Treat your neighbor as though you were made to love each other.

—— Scripture to *Digest* ——

Command those who are rich in this present world not to be arrogant nor to put their hope in wealth, which is so uncertain, but to put their hope in God, who richly provides us with everything for our enjoyment.

Command them to do good, to be rich in good deeds, and to be generous and willing to share. In this way they will lay up treasure for themselves as a firm foundation for the coming age, so that they may take hold of the life that is truly life. (1 Tim. 6:17–19)

Conclusion

This Is Our Place, Our Time

For when we ask whether someone is a good man, we are not asking what he believes, or hopes, but what he loves.

St. Augustine

When right-living people bless the city, it flourishes.

Proverbs 11:11 MSG

I sat at my dining room table, an unusual few minutes of quiet in my house, my four children and husband sleeping, studying, and playing in various corners. My laptop open, I watched the latest news coverage on the hurricane aftermath a few states away. Floodwaters rising and families stranded, calling for help to whoever might come. Everyday heroes showing up to the rescue with rafts, motorboats, and human-powered kayaks. These apparent strangers made human chains a dozen people long that stretched from the shore to cars surrounded by dark, rising waters. The desperate prayers of stranded drivers were answered by neighbors they had never met.

The human chains were not complicated. They were made up of one person holding the arm of another and then another, each link in the chain willing to take on some personal risk in order to get to the terrified person at the end. These fellow citizens knew they were someone else's only hope, so they stepped to the rescue to save that person's life. It was not complicated, but it required true courage.

In my dry dining room, my cheeks were anything but as the tears flowed down them. The willingness to risk one's own safety for a stranger is indeed noble. But something bigger than the power of a good deed was at play in these rescue operations. Care for our neighbor is woven into the very texture of our humanity. God created us for this. As people made in God's image, we long to live out the purposes he has scripted for us.

For the people on my screen, it took a natural disaster, an "act of God," to call them to action. A flood interrupts the busyness of the routine, it breaks habits and ways of always doing things, and it creates urgency. It also creates a way for us to respond with grand, noble gestures, which we tend to like because we can see people rising to meet the occasion. But most days and weeks we are called to love our actual neighbors in the middle of our ordinary lives. No news cameras rolling or record books being kept, only the everyday experiences as the backdrop for us to do something bold and courageous: to love our neighbors as ourselves.

The human chain is needed in these ordinary moments too. Though simple in structure, it requires a collective effort and risk and discomfort to be effective. I've witnessed it, and it is powerful. I've seen it in MOPS groups, when postpartum depression or a preemie baby has landed someone in the hospital and moms have cared for the family still at home. I've seen it at Providence Network, where staff not only have moved into the neighborhood to be with their neighbors who are rebuilding life after domestic violence or addiction, but have moved into the same home, sharing meals and rides and chores as families do. I've seen it on the school playground when a parent's or child's test results have confirmed the worst fears, and tears are wiped, hugs given, and meals made, delivered, and shared, when kids have been picked up and dropped off from school so parents don't have to leave the house. And I've seen it at a bedside, a hospital waiting room, a funeral, and a memorial dedication as presence has mattered. Each person doing their critical part to say we belong to each other.

When I consider my ordinary days, these moments of neighborly love feel most real to me because, well . . . I feel the most intensely in them. My life can become rote; I'm scrambling so much to attend to all the needs of my tribe that I don't have much left to offer anyone else. I want to escape my responsibility here. My urge to avoid my pain or my neighbors' pain leads me down lots of comfort-seeking paths as an escape from the tension of Saturday living. So when I experience neighbors listening rather than ducking the uncomfortable, and giving with open hands, I feel life's richness. It's in those moments of loving my neighbors that I experience the Saturday life, tethered in both pain and hope, the most strongly. It's when I sense, *This is what I was made for.*

If Not Us, Then Who?

It seems in this time of tension and isolation, we the church, the Jesus people, are perfectly positioned to offer the countercultural way of love. Not because it makes us feel better about who we are, but rather because it can be quite uncomfortable. Not because it frees us from awkward positions or conversations, but just the opposite—it makes us live out what we claim to believe about God and his creation. We claim to follow Jesus, and he is clear on what that means. Above all else, we are to love God and our neighbors.

This is not the time for us to be shaking our fists at culture, wondering why someone isn't doing something about _____ (fill in the blank with whatever gets you riled up). It is the time to take up the non-sexy, private, quiet work of loving those God has put in our path.

As Derek and Matt considered the needs of Denver's homeless youth, they asked, "If not us, then who?" They knew they were uniquely positioned to help this given group of neighbors. We are all also uniquely positioned to love someone. The church is positioned to care for humanity. We can each start with those within arm's reach.

In all times and places in the history of the world, our actual neighbors are the ones we find ourselves rubbing up against. Sometimes that rub can feel like friction, but friction creates heat and heat is energy. We don't need to be afraid of the rub. Humanity tends to tribe up, even more so these days. We cluster with people who live like us, believe like us, worship like us, vote like us, and think like us. What if we decided those who lived right in front of us were "our people"? That the very nature of proximity is what defined our tribe?

What if we looked at them as the ones God intended for us to treasure most?

We know Jesus as the incarnational God. He came wrapped in skin in part so people might hear and touch and witness him—the invisible God made visible through a body that "moved into the neighborhood" (John 1:14 MSG). We are living this incarnational life, so we hold to those right here. We hug, high-five, kiss, and dance with our bodies. God made the most intimate union a physical one and chose for life to multiply through this physical connection. And, no surprise, he wants us to love the people in our physical presence. Those within our little world of tangible influence. He knew we'd live in this time and place of virtual relationships and global connection, but his greatest command holds true to love those *physically* right next to us as we love ourselves. Those people we can reach across the fence or the classroom or the traffic lane and touch.

To treasure our neighbors looks like respect—of opinion, belief, choices, and space. We do not force ourselves on our neighbors, just as God does not force himself on us. But with small gestures that can lead to large ones, we are able to offer dignity by how we directly and indirectly treat our neighbors. Those conversations of asking questions and listening, of finding both common and uncommon ground, help us better know, understand, and care for those right in front of us.

This Is Our Place and Time

This is our place. For some reason God placed us on this planet in a unique spot at a unique time. We are living in this point in history in the midst of our actual circumstances.

191

We know from Scripture that God uses the most ordinary, even the most unqualified, candidates to do his work in the world. He carries out his purposes despite us. And so we get over ourselves, both the pride that makes us more self-important than we actually are and our insecurities that we might be the wrong person for the job. Instead, we humbly raise our hands to say, "Here I am, Lord; send me." From the playground to the boardroom, the restaurant kitchen to the big-box store, location does not matter as much as us acknowledging that our location is an opportunity. We may not feel "called" to the place we are—we may even resent that this is our current spot—but our feelings don't dictate God's direction. His command to love our neighbor is true, regardless of our circumstances.

This is also our time. We are the keepers of the gospel, the message of love and hope in the world, for our generation. This is played out in part in how we interact with our neighbors. We have an opportunity to reflect back to them what we believe God says about them. He says they are valuable, known from conception, and they deserve our attention because of their inherent worth. From the way we talk to the gas station attendant in a two-minute interaction to how we care for the elderly neighbor for a decade, we are messengers of human worth and dignity and gospel-centered love.

We live in a time when harsh, divisive words are spoken and shared. When people self-select and are unwillingly placed into categories and camps. Where the tendency to have a litmus test on being friends with someone is increasing. We are splitting, dividing, and splintering. However, we know as God's children that through Christ we are united. "There is neither Jew nor Gentile, neither slave nor free, nor is there male and female, for you are all one in Christ Jesus" (Gal. 3:28). As God's church we can work at unity within the walls of our buildings and the borders of our hearts. We can also demonstrate this worldview through the barriers we are willing to step over in Jesus's name. Words are empty without actions, and no actions speak louder than a countercultural move toward holding the tension of difference and loving anyway.

We have this God-gifted thing we call "free will," the ability to make choices within the constraints of our actual lives. We can choose to take a posture of humility, to ask questions and sincerely listen, to be in the uncomfortable and not try to change what we cannot, to bring warmth and generosity to our neighbors. No matter the location—apartment to cul-de-sac, city block to country road—God has given us choices in these matters. It is our time to make them. He has also remarkably given us the choice to live out these practices with our neighbors regardless of who we are and who they are. It may be easier for some of us than others to practice the practices, but we always have the choice.

My brothers and sisters, the world is eager, desperate, for the love of Christ demonstrated through us. We are not arriving to save our neighbors but to demonstrate his love with open hands and hearts, so that they may know what we profess to believe: they are created in God's image, seen by him, and loved by him. Let us exercise that glorious free will and choose to express to our neighbors to the best of our imperfect, human-constrained abilities how high and wide and deep is the love of Christ.

The Conclusion to the Conclusion

"Teacher, which is the greatest commandment in the Law?"

Jesus replied: "'Love the Lord your God with all your heart and with all your soul and with all your mind.' This is the first and greatest commandment. And the second is like it: 'Love your neighbor as yourself.' All the Law and the Prophets hang on these two commandments." (Matt. 22:36–40)

We end right where we started: "All the Law and the Prophets hang on these two commandments." All that matters in how we conduct ourselves is summed up right here. May we be people who take this business of loving our neighbors seriously, knowing God does. With all of the humility we can muster, we join our Maker to treasure the people right in front of us so that they may experience the hope of Christ through us. This often difficult, hilarious, beautiful, uncomfortable, life-giving, glorious work of loving our neighbors in the here and now, in the midst of our actual lives, is Saturday living.

—— Questions for *Reflection* ——

1. How are you uniquely positioned to love your neighbors?
2. Who is right within arm's reach to care for? Whom would you like to know more in order to love more?
3. How does Saturday living actualize in your life? With your neighbors?
4. What would treasuring your neighbors look like in the next week? The next month? The next year?

5. How does the charge to love your neighbor impact your plan for today?

Scripture to *Digest*

So now faith, hope, and love abide, these three; but the greatest of these is love. (1 Cor. 13:13 ESV)

More Ways to Connect with Your Neighbors

All will concede that in order to have good neighbors,
we must also be good neighbors. That applies in every
field of human endeavor.

Harry S. Truman

Additional Ideas for Practicing the Practices

How you practice each of the seven practices is as unique as you, your actual circumstances, and your actual neighbors. These additional ideas are not exhaustive lists, nor are they meant to be prescriptive. Rather, these are ideas to get you started as you consider what it means to ask questions or lighten up in the context of your actual life. Because you know *your* circumstances, *your* neighbors, and *your*self. So consider how God might be asking you to implement these practices in your daily experiences—and go and love your neighbors like only you can.

Holding a Posture of Humility

1. Remember who God is and who you are in context to him.

2. Walk, sit, and stand with good posture. Consider your humility as you consider your posture.

3. Play praise music while cleaning or driving. Worship God in your daily tasks.

4. Make a list of all the ways your neighbors are made in God's image.

5. Ask a trusted friend for feedback on your areas of potential pride.

6. Pray for a neighbor you wouldn't have chosen as a neighbor.

7. Rake your neighbor's leaves or shovel their sidewalk as a surprise gift.

8. Be mindful of your expectations of your neighbors, especially when you do something for them.

9. Avoid offering your qualifications or accomplishments in conversation.

10. Ask God to reveal unseen biases or assumptions about your neighbors.

Asking Questions to Learn

1. Set an alarm to follow up with a neighbor about something they mentioned earlier.

2. Go on social media with the intent of asking questions about others' posts.

3. Research a news story that doesn't impact you but does impact one of your neighbors.

4. Attend a cultural event or community meeting with the goal of learning three new things.

5. Subscribe to a periodical or blog that addresses a new topic that impacts your neighbors.

6. Stand in front of a mirror and practice relaxing your face. Have someone tell you shocking things as you practice.

7. Slow your breathing and lower your voice during conversation.

8. Watch a documentary on a topic that is new to you.

9. Use follow-up language such as, "Tell me more about . . ."

10. Include open-ended questions for God when praying for your neighbors.

Being Quiet to Listen

1. Take a social media fast for a finite amount of time.

2. Sit in quiet and solitude for five minutes a day. No music or reading.

3. Go on a prayer walk around your neighborhood or apartment building.

4. Make note of your neighbors' dress, habits, and preferences.

5. Try "listening" with all the senses. What do you hear, see, feel, smell, and taste as you walk through your neighborhood?

6. Put your phone in a place out of arm's reach (your purse, car, house) when talking with your neighbors.

7. Shut your mouth. Simply do not talk when someone else is talking. (Psst—this is also known as interrupting.)

8. Resist the urge to share details about your neighbors. (Psst—this is also known as gossip.)

9. Set an alarm on your phone to pray daily or throughout the day for various neighbors.

10. Ask God how you might better love your neighbors. Then listen for his response.

Standing in the Awkward

1. Allow yourself to feel uncomfortable.

2. Admit out loud when you learn you are wrong.

3. Challenge a systemic problem by offering constructive help (not just criticism).

4. Pursue the awkward by introducing yourself to everyone in your pew at church, the pickup line at school, or the bank.

5. Go out of your way to meet a neighbor thirty years older or younger than you. Challenge yourself to find two common interests.

6. Pray for discernment in when to stay and when to go in a situation or relationship.

7. Hold the tension for other people by being the neutral person in a confrontation or reconciliation.

8. Admit out loud when things are feeling weird.

9. Be honest in your disagreements. (Note: this does not mean judgy or nasty.)

10. Invite other people into already uncomfortable situations (help them get practice in the practice too).

Accepting What Is

1. Make a plan to encourage one of your neighbors.

2. Walk, run, or skip through your neighborhood. Get some exercise so you can offer your best self when loving your neighbors.

3. Join a group that is already loving your neighbors the way you would like to.

4. When presented with an opportunity, ask yourself, *Am I the only one who can do this?*

5. Answer the phone or door when a neighbor calls. Allow yourself to be interrupted.

6. Get sufficient sleep.

7. When feeling conflicted about your neighbor's decisions, validate their feelings.

8. Pray, meditate on, and read Scripture. Keep your spiritual life healthy.

9. When tempted to offer a neighbor a solution, ask yourself, *Is this a time for me to accept what is and simply be with them in this moment?*

10. Love the people you are serving alongside. They are your neighbors too.

Lightening Up

1. Designate one night a week or month as a time to have the same (or different) neighbors over for dinner.

2. Deliver flowers (or fruit or homemade cards) to your neighbors.

3. Smile and start a conversation in places where people congregate to wait: the post office, the grocery store, the DMV.

4. Bring muffins to the school secretary, doughnuts to the gas station attendant, and burritos to the office maintenance crew.

5. Practice kindness and courtesy. Hold the door open at the grocery store, wave to your neighbor walking her dog, let someone go ahead of you in traffic.

6. Compliment someone serving you as part of their job. Bonus: ask to speak to their boss to pass the compliment on to the one who gives raises.

7. Laugh at yourself. Don't be afraid to see the silliness or ridiculousness in some of the things you do. Don't be afraid to let others see it either.

8. Bring a neighbor a gift of something you both love: coffee, geraniums, comic books. Something that says, "I remember we share this."

9. Make a list of the qualities you appreciate about that hard-to-love neighbor.

10. Throw a party in someone's honor. Likely you have a coworker, a neighbor, or someone who works hard on your behalf who could use a "thank you."

Giving Freely

1. Replace your weekly luxury spending (dinner out, a new shirt) with spending on your neighbors. Buy them something that you may consider frivolous but is meaningful to them.

2. Thank God for the life he has given you. Ask him how you can use it today to be a blessing to someone else.

3. Choose to extend grace when you feel anger or frustration creep up toward a neighbor, even if you feel you are in the right.

4. Offer some of your living space for your neighbors' use: your garden, your playroom, your piano. What could your neighbors come over and use with joy?

5. Pray for your neighbors' specific circumstances. Tell them you're praying if you feel comfortable doing so.

6. Ask for forgiveness quickly and frequently.

7. Leave gift cards to a neighborhood restaurant or grocery store in your neighbor's mailbox.

8. Commit a full day to caring for your neighbors: childcare, yard work, driving them to appointments. Block off the time so you don't spend it somewhere else.

9. Determine your unique skills that have value in the marketplace. Determine a way you can use those skills for a neighbor who needs them.

10. Pray, "Lord, send me," and see where, or more importantly to whom, he sends you.

Ten Ways to Connect with Families throughout the Year

Whether it's your apartment common room, your living room, or your church basement, you can use almost any place to bring people together if you have a common purpose. It doesn't need to be fancy; in fact, it's better if it isn't, then it's less intimidating and more likely to inspire a neighbor to try the hosting next time around. Here are a few ways to connect with your young and young-at-heart neighbors.

1. Snow forts and hot cocoa. Can we all agree we tend to overcomplicate hospitality? Pinterest and Instagram haven't done us any favors in this department. If it's snowy, send everyone to the front yard, knock on some doors, invite them to make snow forts, and call them in for cocoa afterward. Snow party . . . done!

2. Valentine making. This is the best way to finish up half-used craft supplies. You can do a craft whether you are two or ninety-two, on a holiday where it's almost impossible to offend anyone. Show your neighbors a little love by offering them a way to show someone else some love. Glitter preferred.

3. Easter egg hunt. Why is it that finding plastic-colored eggs in the grass is so fun? The only prep required: filling eggs and mowing the lawn. Want to make it a multiple connection kind of thing? Host an egg-dyeing party the day before. Because nothing says "resurrection" like the smell of vinegar and sulfur.

4. Last day of school. Parents may be dreading this day, but kids everywhere are celebrating. Water balloons, popsicles, and a slip 'n' slide seem like the perfect way to inaugurate summer. This is a great time to make plans with neighbors for the rest of the summer or invite kids to VBS.

5. Fourth of July fireworks (or other national celebration if you are outside the US). We want to look for unifying celebrations. If you are living in this country, likely you want to celebrate that fact. You could go the nostalgia route with watermelon, gunnysack races, and pony rides, or the emergency room route with sparklers, smoke bombs, and Roman candles.

6. First day of school. Who doesn't love a new notebook and No. 2 pencil? Okay, maybe not everyone, but we can all feel the excitement of a new year and new beginnings. Have pancakes before (or ice cream sandwiches after) the first day of classes. Ask all of the adults to share about their favorite teacher. This involves neighbors who may not have kids in school.

7. Trick-or-treating. What other day of the year do your neighbors (perhaps in the tens, perhaps in the hundreds) come knocking on your door? Make your home memorable. Give out generous portions, creative prizes, and lots of praise for costumes. This is an opportunity to tell your neighbors you care for them regardless of your like or dislike for the holiday.

8. Parade and pie. If you're in a neighborhood where lots of people stay in town for Thanksgiving, make the morning memorable by having pie and coffee for anyone not guarding—I mean cooking—the turkey. Turn on the Macy's Thanksgiving Day Parade, and you've got an event.

9. Christmas chaos. From caroling parties to light-decorating contests (mostly unofficial), neighborhoods offer all kinds of opportunities to connect during the season. Host a gift-wrapping party (no kids allowed), or bring Santa to the neighborhood (kids of any age welcome). From cookies to cards, there are lots of holiday treats you can leave for your neighbors.

10. Progressive dinner. Why not move the party from one person's house to everyone's house? On New Year's Eve, or any eve, a dinner that moves course to course and location to location can be done by foot, bike, or car. Our church hosts a dinner that starts and ends in our building and sends groups out to various houses for the main course (all preplanned and approved, of course).

Ten Ways to Love Your Homebound Neighbors

The ability to be up and moving and get out of the house can be impacted by many factors. Age can keep our bodies from working and moving. Illness can keep someone in bed or quarantined from the world of germs. A physical or other disability can create limitations. Even having a newborn who needs to eat every ninety minutes or a child who is sick can keep an able-bodied parent stuck inside. Whatever the reason and however long the season of being homebound, we as neighbors can offer some practical help to those right in front of us.

1. Shovel snow (and mow in the summer and rake leaves in the fall). That yard and sidewalk may be a source of stress for someone who can't care for them, and a snowy driveway can make some people nervous about getting out in an emergency. Use your able body to love your neighbor in a practical way.

209

2. Engage in conversation. Well, we know asking questions gives us insights and good information (see chapter 2), but conversation alone can help keep someone sane. Maybe what your neighbor needs most is company—someone to sit and talk with them about *whatever*. Being at home can sometimes limit a person's range of topics, but there's always the news and the weather.

3. Grocery shop or run other errands for them. If you are already headed to the grocery store or post office, ask if they need anything. Better yet, ask if they'd like to join you. Depending on their situation, simply getting out of the house may be the most important errand on their to-do list.

4. Offer tech support. Does your neighbor know how to listen to audiobooks? To video conference with her children? To record his favorite shows? If something comes up in conversation and you know of some technology that might help a neighbor feel less isolated, offer to help get it set up. This may be most helpful for those on the senior end of the spectrum.

5. Get out to vote. Does your neighbor need a ride to the polls or to have their ballot dropped off? This is a great way to say they matter to the larger community, especially if you have different political views.

6. Share a recipe. Food is the great unifier. We all eat. Use it as a place of common ground. Whether in your kitchen or your neighbor's, sharing a family recipe or other tradition can get the stories going and spark lots of great conversation, not to mention lots of yummy food. On the practical end, make extras to stock your neighbor's fridge with their favorite treat.

7. Bring stuff in. Mail, Amazon deliveries, and groceries must go from the porch or car into the house or apartment.

Keep your eye out and don't wait to be asked. Everyone can use a little kindness on a regular basis.

8. Feed them. Are you just one person? Make a little extra of what you're already having for dinner and run it across the street. Is it for a family who needs to eat? Double what you're making. Extras in the freezer are always good. You don't need an organized meal train to step in and say, "How about I bring dinner over?" People have been doing it since long before there were online sign-ups.

9. Entertain them. Being stuck at home can be *bor-ing*. Pick up their library order, bring over a deck of cards, grab some new toys to explore. Both grown-ups and kids need a little fun. If there are kids in the house, offer to babysit them in their home or yours. Stir-crazy is especially crazy for little people with lots of energy.

10. Care for their pets. Does the dog need to be walked? Is the fish food running low? Does the kitty need to make a visit to the vet? Animals can be the best companions for our homebound neighbors, offering comfort and snuggles. Caring for our neighbors' furry friends is an indirect way of caring for them.

Ten Reasons to Have a Block (or Street or Building) Party

Whether you want to meet your neighbors, make stronger connections, or just have fun together, having a time and place plus a purpose or a theme helps rally the troops. You can go all out or keep it simple—whatever fits your personality and your group's needs best. In fact, have a planning committee or team. Working together to make the party happen is a party unto itself. Spending time together is essential to knowing your neighbors. Gathering neighbors to meet each other is a gift you can give with exponential benefits. So get creative and find reasons to celebrate. Together.

1. A local sports team. Whether it's a pro or college team, if your neighbors want to cheer them on, do it together. An outdoor pregame tailgate party with the grills fired is an easy way to gather people. Game watching can then be together or separate, but together is always more fun.

2. The season. It doesn't matter the season, there is something to celebrate. Have pumpkins delivered in the fall and carve them together. Turn on everyone's front sprinklers in the summer for a huge sprinkler obstacle course. Celebrate what makes the season special.

3. A shared accomplishment. The construction on the street is done? The apartment building remodel is complete? You survived it together; now celebrate together. Maybe you worked together on something—a community garden or a playset installation. Whether someone else did the work or your very hands did, it's a reason for a party.

4. A new arrival to or departure from the neighborhood. The passage of people in and out of your community can be marked together. Don't make the new family do the work of meeting neighbors; have them meet you all at once. And give those leaving a proper farewell, letting them know they will be missed.

5. Your local heroes. Police and firefighters, mail carriers and sanitation workers. Some of the same people serve you and your neighbors as part of their work. Coming together to thank them collectively can have an exponential impact on the appreciation you offer.

6. Shared profit. Combine a party with a block garage sale, or throw the party when the garages are closed up at the end of the day. You can always designate a shared charity to give a portion of the day's sales to, creating a sense of shared mission, and/or you can pool profits to order takeout.

7. A single person. Every person matters, so it's okay to have a party in someone's honor. A birthday is always good, or a graduation. A new job is worth celebrating, and so is a new baby. When the group comes together around a single person or family, you reinforce the importance and contribution of every member of your community, and the love is magnified.

8. A beginning or an end. School is starting or summer is. School is ending or summer is. Having a kickoff event helps you plan for the sports season, school year, or temperature change. It's a great way to promote community for what's ahead. Closing a season can also call for celebration as you remember the hard work and/or fun you've shared.

9. Food. Food alone is a reason to come together. It's the great equalizer, after all. Have a cook-off that is competitive and themed (like chili or dessert) with judges and categories. Give prizes and assign the categories based on what best reflects the spirit of your block or building. This party can be more laid-back and called a potluck. That works too.

10. Plain old fun. From a soccer game in the street to popsicles on the front stoop, you don't need an excuse to have fun together. A party also doesn't need to be elaborate; in fact, the simpler the better, because then it can be more regular. No need to spend lots of money or energy. A group effort can make the workload easy for all and increase everyone's investment in the outcome: fun!

Acknowledgments

It is in the spirit of teamwork and neighborly love that so many have contributed to this book.

To anyone who has a story in these pages, I owe a huge thank-you. My circles of real-life people are my strongest source of inspiration. To Dave Runyon, Patricia Raybon, Karen Parks, Elisa Morgan, and Jeff Johnsen, a special thank-you for taking time to talk through this topic before the writing started. To Annie Rim, Steve Garcia, Terri Conlin, Ruth Olsson, Carol Kuykendall, Krista Gilbert, Wes Scheu, Jennifer Wilson, Kristin Williams, Kendra Grabowski, and Kendra Tillman, a thank-you for reading excerpts and offering feedback. You all love your neighbors well, and I appreciate your input.

To the teams at William K. Jensen Literary Agency and Baker Books, thank you for believing we need to do a better job at loving our neighbors and that I might have something to say about this topic. And to Liz Heaney, a special thank-you for ordering my words (and my paragraphs) to help me articulate what I'm truly intending to say.

To my real-life neighbors near and far, I appreciate all I have learned from watching you.

And to my family, thank you for giving me opportunities to interact with God's world. You are my best instruments of introduction to new people and places. Because of your work, school, soccer, sidewalk chalk, and general need for groceries, I am pushed out of my self-selected circles to meet my neighbors. I love you.

To God be the glory. We love because he first loved us.

Notes

Introduction

1. Kim Parker et al., "How Urban, Suburban, and Rural Residents Interact with Their Neighbors," Pew Research Center, May 22, 2018, http://www.pewsocialtrends.org/2018/05/22/how-urban-suburban-and-rural-residents-interact-with-their-neighbors/.

2. G. Oscar Anderson, "Loneliness among Older Adults: A National Survey of Adults 45+," AARP, September 2010, https://www.aarp.org/research/topics/life/info-2014/loneliness_2010.html.

3. Julianne Holt-Lunstad, "So Lonely I Could Die," American Psychological Association, August 5, 2017, http://www.apa.org/news/press/releases/2017/08/lonely-die.aspx.

4. "2 Peter," Biblica, accessed August 28, 2018, https://www.biblica.com/resources/scholar-notes/niv-study-bible/intro-to-2-peter/.

5. Tony Campolo, "It's Friday but Sunday's Coming," https://tonycampolo.org/its-friday-but-sundays-coming/.

Chapter 1 Holding a Posture of Humility

1. John Frank, "Why It's So Hard to Define Where You Can Legally Smoke Pot in Colorado," *Denver Post*, May 18, 2017, https://www.denverpost.com/2017/05/18/legally-smoking-pot-colorado/.

2. Eugene Cho, *Overrated: Are We More in Love with the Idea of Changing the World Than Actually Changing the World?* (Colorado Springs: David C. Cook, 2014), 137.

3. "The Healthy Way Series: What Healthy Relationships Do and Don't Have," January 23, 2018, in *The Open Door Sisterhood*, podcast, http://theopendoorsisterhood.com/2018/01/23/the-healthy-way-series-getting-right-in-relationships/.

4. Rick Warren, *The Purpose Driven Life: What on Earth Am I Here For?* (Grand Rapids: Zondervan, 2002), 148.

5. Sarah Young, *Jesus Always: Embracing Joy in His Presence* (Nashville: Thomas Nelson, 2016), 22.

6. Adele Ahlberg Calhoun, *Spiritual Disciplines Handbook: Practices That Transform Us* (Downers Grove, IL: InterVarsity Press, 2005), 12.

Chapter 2 Asking Questions to Learn

1. Frank Sesno, *Ask More: The Power of Questions to Open Doors, Uncover Solutions, and Spark Change* (New York: AMACOM, 2017), 56.

2. Sesno, 198.

3. Jeff Thompson, "Is Nonverbal Communication a Numbers Game?," *Psychology Today*, September 10, 2011, https://www.psychologytoday.com/us/blog/beyond-words/201109/is-nonverbal-communication-numbers-game.

4. David S. Matsumoto, "Speaking of Psychology: Nonverbal Communication Speaks Volumes," *American Psychological Association*, accessed October 15, 2018, http://www.nonverbalgroup.com/2011/08/how-much-of-communication-is-really-nonverbal.

5. David Livermore, *Leading with Cultural Intelligence: The Real Secret to Success* (New York: AMACOM, 2015), 116.

Chapter 3 Being Quiet to Listen

1. Calhoun, *Spiritual Disciplines Handbook*, 108.

2. "Daily Time Spent on Social Networking by Internet Users Worldwide from 2012 to 2017 (in Minutes)," Statista, accessed August 30, 2018, https://www.statista.com/statistics/433871/daily-social-media-usage-worldwide/.

3. Alexandra Kuykendall, *Loving My Actual Life: An Experiment in Relishing What's Right in Front of Me* (Grand Rapids: Baker Books, 2016), 23–39.

4. Malcom Gladwell, *Blink: The Power of Thinking without Thinking* (New York: Hachette Book Group, 2005), 154–55.

5. Nancy F. Clark, "10 Steps to Effective Listening," *Forbes*, September 11, 2012, https://www.forbes.com/sites/womensmedia/2012/11/09/10-steps-to-effective-listening/#5b6a56653891.

6. See Calhoun, *Spiritual Disciplines Handbook*.

Chapter 4 Standing in the Awkward

1. Jefferson Bethke, foreword to *Tables in the Wilderness: A Memoir of God Found, Lost, and Found Again*, by Preston Yancey (Grand Rapids: Zondervan, 2014), 12.

Chapter 6 Lightening Up

1. Scott Weems, "The Science behind Why We Laugh, and the Funniest Joke in the World," *Huffington Post*, May 4, 2014, https://www.huffingtonpost.com/scott-weems/joke-book_b_4892644.html.

Chapter 7 Giving Freely

1. "Giving Thanks Can Make You Happier," Harvard Health Publishing, accessed September 5, 2018, https://www.health.harvard.edu/healthbeat/giving-thanks-can-make-you-happier; Melanie Greenberg, "How Gratitude Leads to a Happier Life," *Psychology Today*, November 22, 2015, https://www.psychologytoday.com/us/blog/the-mindful-self-express/201511/how-gratitude-leads-happier-life.

Alexandra Kuykendall spends her days driving to multiple schools, figuring out what to feed her people, and searching for a better solution to the laundry dilemma. Author of *Loving My Actual Life*, *Loving My Actual Christmas*, and *The Artist's Daughter*, Alex is cohostess of *The Open Door Sisterhood* podcast. A trusted voice for today's Christian women, she speaks around the world on issues of parenting, faith, and identity. She lives in the shadows of downtown Denver with her husband, Derek, and their four daughters. You can connect with her at AlexandraKuykendall.com.

ALSO AVAILABLE FROM

Alexandra Kuykendall

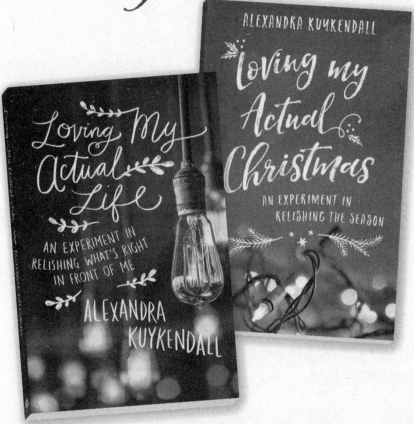

CONNECT WITH

Alex

ALEXANDRAKUYKENDALL.COM

Alex_Kuykendall

AlexandraKuykendall.Author

AlexandraKuykendall

TheOpenDoorSisterhood.com

LIKE THIS BOOK?

Consider sharing it with others!

- Share or mention the book on your social media platforms. Use the hashtag **#LovingMyActualNeighbor**.

- Write a book review on your blog or on a retailer site.

- Pick up a copy for friends, family, or strangers— anyone who you think would enjoy and be challenged by its message!

- Recommend this book for your church, workplace, book club, or class.

- Follow Baker Books and Alexandra Kuykendall on social media and tell us what you like about the book.

f	ReadBakerBooks	f	AlexandraKuykendall.Author
🐦	ReadBakerBooks	🐦	Alex_Kuykendall
📷	ReadBakerBooks	📷	AlexandraKuykendall